ONE MAN'S IRELAND

Memoirs of Dan Mulvihill, Maverick Republican

Owen O'Shea

First published in 2025 by
Merrion Press
10 George's Street
Newbridge
Co. Kildare
Ireland
www.merrionpress.ie

978 1 78537 545 3 (Paper)
978 1 78537 551 4 (eBook)

A CIP catalogue record for this book is
available from the British Library.

Typeset in Calluna 11/17 pt

Cover design by Fiachra McCarthy

Merrion Press is a member of Publishing Ireland.

CONTENTS

ACKNOWLEDGEMENTS

THIS IS THE STORY of an Irish republican, a freedom fighter, a maverick, a writer of letters, an advocate for old friends, an adjudicator, a man of principle.

It is the story of a man from my home parish who, until now, was a largely forgotten figure in the history of Ireland and its emergence from the grip of the British Empire over a century ago.

This is Dan Mulvihill's story, in his own words, and supplemented by other archive material.

To enable it to be told, I am immensely grateful to the team at Merrion Press, particularly managing director, Conor Graham, as well as Síne Quinn and Wendy Logue, and copyeditor, Heidi Houlihan.

My thanks too to the many archivists, librarians and independent researchers who pointed me in the direction of additional sources.

The Mulvihill family graciously supported this publication.

Finally, my immense and enduring gratitude to Celia, Peadar, Neasa and Aodhán for continuing to indulge my passion for history.

A NOTE ON SOURCES

THE MAIN SOURCE FOR this work is the unpublished memoir of Dan Mulvihill. Quotations from the memoir are not given endnotes. All other sources are fully referenced.

PROLOGUE

Brackhill

THE MECHANICAL TICK OF the clock punctured the silence in the kitchen of the modest farmhouse at Brackhill, half a mile from Castlemaine in the centre of County Kerry, the pendulum swaying in time with each turn of the cog. The cry of newborn lambs in a nearby field crept in through the open window. The cold rain had stopped falling but there was still a biting chill in the air. The cups and saucers remained in the sink, unwashed. The day's post remained unopened. Dan Mulvihill hauled the Smith-Corona typewriter from the sideboard to the table in the middle of the room. A few blank pages were retrieved from the cabinet in the sitting room. He sighed as he moved the pile of newspapers on the table out of the way and pulled the chair closer as he blew the dust off the keys. The 'G' and the 'H' on the old typewriter often jammed and had to be prised back into place with a finger, but he was used to that, even if the creep of arthritis made it more difficult of late. Dan knew that a letter like this had to be typed rather than written by hand. It was a letter he had been ready to compose for the past few weeks.

A few of the neighbours, who had been visiting, had just left. Condolences had been shared over a pot of strong tea and iced buns. 'Sorry for your troubles, Dan.' 'She had a long life, God rest her.' 'Ninety-one, wasn't it a great age?' They meant well, the neighbours. They were decent, honest and hard-working people who, like the Mulvihills, had farmed the fertile land on the banks of the River Maine for generations. The womenfolk would keen over the remains at the wake later that evening just as their ancestors had done for hundreds of years.

It was 21 March 1981 and Mulvihill's beloved sister, Catherine – who was always better-known as Katie and with whom he had lived alone for many years on the family farm – had finally succumbed to old age the previous day at Killarney District Hospital. When the phone call had come, it was no surprise. She had barely known him the last time he visited. Her breathing was laboured, her sleep deeper than before. There was little more he could do. They had moved her to a room of her own about ten days ago, knowing that her time was limited. 'She didn't suffer, Mr Mulvihill,' the matron had told him down the phone line. 'It was peaceful.' The news of her death stunned him nonetheless, the realisation that she would never come home again to occupy her customary perch beside the fireplace, leaving him alone to live out his years, surrounded by his teeming library of books, letters, video cassettes and newspapers.

Though her deafness had slowly taken its toll on conversation between the pair, Katie was ever curious and engaged.

Before her deteriorating health had forced her to stay for a prolonged period in the hospital, Dan had become accustomed to turning up the volume on the television more and more, especially for the evening news. She was good company even though she had become feeble. He had come to do more and more of the household chores and all the cooking.

Theirs had always been more than the normal brother–sister relationship. Of all their siblings, Dan and Katie had most in common. They had become close when tuberculosis took their brother in 1919, when they were only teenagers. There were nearly six years between them, but for as long as Dan could remember, they had been kindred spirits, fiery and fun in equal measure, running the fields near the river and pushing each other into the nettles and into the water for devilment.

The close bond had been forged in other ways too: the pair also had a shared politics and a shared involvement in the fight for Irish independence. Dan may have been the high-profile and charismatic leader of the Irish Republican Army (IRA), the close friend of Éamon de Valera, the man beaten up and jailed by the Staters, and the leader of men in the ambushes that pockmarked the history of Ireland in the early 1920s, but Katie was as integral to the revolution in Ireland as her brother, even if her involvement in Cumann na mBan and her work in support of the IRA went largely unknown and unacknowledged for so many years.

It was Katie who had made the buckshot for the gun Dan had used at Ballymacandy; it was she who had cooked for and clothed Tom and Charlie Dálaigh when Mulvihill's was one of the only safe houses left; it was she who hid the £350 they used to buy guns in England; it was she who cooked dinner for Liam Lynch when he was the most wanted man in Ireland; and it was she who cycled undetected through so many checkpoints on the road to Killorglin, ensuring that the men in Glencar received news of a looming round-up.

The pair might not have talked much about those days for many years, but Katie never lost the republican spark. Dan noticed her paying closer attention than usual to the TV news on RTÉ whenever Don Cockburn solemnly imparted the latest tragedies of the Troubles in Northern Ireland, when they started the campaign for civil rights in Derry, or when Jack Lynch looked into the camera and pledged to support the Catholics in the North. If she was able, he thought, Katie would have been the first one over the border to fight with them.

The moment the phone call with the matron had ended, Dan instinctively thought of the many practical matters that follow any bereavement: the wake, the prayers, the sandwiches, the Mass. But one of those tasks was urgent and paramount: notifying the Department of Defence that Katie had passed on. He knew the address well: it wasn't the first letter Dan had sent to the department in his countless years lobbying for pensions for his comrades, pleading with ministers to reverse so many of the decisions to deny those men and women an allowance, detailing the many ambushes and shootings his men and women had been involved in, offering references, maps, names, dates.

A steady path had been worn to the door at Brackhill by the men of the Old IRA – and plenty of the women of Cumann na mBan too – when they were applying for their pension, and Dan was forced to reach for the typewriter each time there was a knock at the door. Despite plenty of angry missives to officials and his frustration with the labyrinthine bureaucracy involved in getting a few pounds for those who had fought for their country, Dan knew that the bureaucratic wheels kept turning. He knew that Katie's hard-won pension cheque for her efforts during the war would be stopped following her passing. Easier to tell the department now and get the next cheque cancelled than wait for it to come in the post and owe them money, because, as he had learned on so many occasions, Hell hath no fury like a government department that is owed money.

Dan composed himself for a moment, rolling a blank page into position. He turned the platen knob as the paper clicked into place. He paused. The headlines in *The Irish Press* on the table beside him caught his eye: 'UDR kill youth in car chase' read one, 'IRA killing condemned' read another. Bobby Sands had been refusing food for twenty days and Thatcher wasn't budging. The daily accounts of murder and mayhem from Northern Ireland were nothing new, but they had a resonance this morning. What would Katie make of the hunger strikes, he pondered, or Dan's comrades of old, many of whom had died for Ireland? Would they be remembered like Bobby Sands?

He began to punch the keys on the typewriter, the 'clack, clack, clack' echoing through the kitchen.

Brackhill,
Castlemaine,
21 March 1981.

A cara [*sic*],

My sister who was in receipt of C na Mbann [*sic*] Pension and Special Allowance, died yesterday, 20th March. Let me know what the procedure is. Do you require a death Cert. I am the only one of the family left alive.

D. Mulvihill.

P.S. She was in Hospital in Killarney for the past few years. Her Pension and Allowance was being paid to [the] Hospital.

D. M.

He turned the knob and peeled the letter from the top of the typewriter. Squinting at the print, he retrieved an envelope from the top drawer in the dresser and wrote on the envelope: 'Department of Defence, Finance Branch, Dublin'. He would post the letter in Milltown on his way to see Fr Quane. Pay the priest now for the funeral Mass so there would be no fuss afterwards, he thought. Katie would be buried in the family plot at Rath cemetery in Tralee. He needed to phone the undertaker. He would ring him from the village.

He glanced towards Katie's armchair near the fireplace, her shawl draped over one arm and the dent in the cushions still there as if she had only been gone an hour. Donning his cap and overcoat, he pulled the back door firmly closed behind him.

INTRODUCTION

'One Man's Ireland'

DAN MULVIHILL WAS A man of letters but not in the conventional sense. Over the course of many decades, he wrote hundreds, maybe thousands, of letters, which form part of the tapestry of correspondence and documentation that records Ireland's revolutionary years. The letters, many of which are threaded through these pages, were churned out of the same typewriter on which Mulvihill wrote of his sister Katie's demise in 1981. It was also on the same typewriter that he wrote the manuscript which forms the basis of this book, a memoir which tells of his life as a 'maverick' republican – as he often described himself – over several decades. Written in the late 1970s and supplemented with a few additional details and annotations into the early 1980s, it is one of the very few first-hand accounts of the years of revolution in Ireland. And for almost half a century, it remained unpublished.

It wasn't until the end of the 1970s that Dan Mulvihill began to write his memoir. Why did he wait so long? Other

IRA men, nationally recognised household names like Dan Breen, Tom Barry, Ernie O'Malley and a handful of Kerry IRA veterans, published their accounts soon after the revolution and cemented their place in the nation's history, becoming iconic figures in the pantheon of Irish republican heroes. But Mulvihill waited until the winter of his life to record his memories and anecdotes. Did events in his later years compel him to document what he had suffered in the name of Ireland? Mulvihill had no immediate family and, with Katie, the last of his surviving siblings, in deteriorating health, maybe it was time to leave his testimony behind. Was he simply putting on paper the memories of bygone days while his mind was still clear and as the end of his life approached?

It wasn't as if Mulvihill had adopted the stance that exemplified the approach of many of his comrades to talking about the troubled times. A veil of silence often prevailed among combatants, the relatives of the dead and the civilians caught up in the fighting. Some things were too painful to speak of. But Mulvihill, according to those who asked him, never hesitated in talking about the wars in which he soldiered, whether it was recounting tales of fighting the Black and Tans, the last time he saw Harry Boland, the burning of Fermoy Barracks, the hunger strikes, the blood-soaked floors in Mountjoy Prison, or the verbal tirades of the Free State soldiers. But as the years went on, there was less and less interest in his tales of heroism and bravery. Time was moving on. The new generation wasn't very interested in the wars of 1919 to 1923. There was a new war now – this time in Northern Ireland. But something in Mulvihill, despite his advancing years, felt compelled to put pen to paper, to document his life and times, to record his part in Ireland's revolution.

Mulvihill had every intention of publishing his memoir, a 20,000-word chronology and series of anecdotes of his life and times. A recently unearthed recording of an interview with him demonstrates his intention to publish, even though it was something he never achieved in his lifetime. Less than a year before he died, in 1984, Mulvihill was interviewed by David Rae and his son, Stephen, an interview which only came to light while this author was writing the story of the Ballymacandy ambush of 1921.[1]

David Rae, from Boolteens, Castlemaine, was a son of a prominent IRA leader from the 1920s who was a close friend and ally of Mulvihill during their fight for Irish independence. Stephen Rae senior, David's father, was an intelligence officer with the IRA in Keel, a large rural parish at the eastern end of the Dingle Peninsula. The Rae family was steeped in republicanism and their hotel at Boolteens was a haven for IRA men on the run. As David and Stephen Rae junior sat down to speak with Mulvihill in his kitchen in Brackhill in 1984, the interviewee was reticent and was in bad form: 'Nobody does an interview with me,' Mulvihill declared petulantly. Within moments, however, he was fully engaged, describing the memoir he had recently completed:

> It covers the day I left Brackhill in 1916 to 1977. There are three copies of it in America. I was in very bad humour in

> 1974/75 when I wrote it when things were going bad. Con Casey heard about it, and he wanted to publish it, but they wouldn't publish the end of it, and I had an awful job of getting it [back] off him. He wanted to keep it you see.[2]

Con Casey from Tralee was one of the leading figures in the Kerry IRA during the War of Independence and the Civil War. His wife, Susan Dálaigh, was a member of the well-known republican family of Knockaneacoolteen near Firies, whose brothers included Charlie, who was executed at Drumboe in County Donegal during the Civil War. The Dálaigh family and Dan Mulvihill had operated hand in glove in the fight against the British. In later life, Casey became a reporter with *The Kerryman* newspaper, where he was editor for fifteen years until his retirement in 1974.[3] He regarded his work as a journalist as a way of keeping 'the flag of Irish culture and nationalism flying'.[4]

Casey's approach to Mulvihill about publishing his account originated not only in their shared involvement in what became known as the 'Old IRA' but also stemmed from Casey's work as a publisher of accounts of the revolutionary years in Kerry and beyond. On hearing that Mulvihill had compiled a memoir, he was very interested, as Mulvihill recalled:

> He sent out Andy Cooney's son to me then about six months after. Cooney is dead, he was a doctor in America, he was a pal of mine, he was chief of staff [of the IRA]

> in the 1930s.[5] He [his son] landed here to me … Do you remember the bank strike? 1976 … the strike was on when he came. And [he] said would I give him the loan of it, and he kept it and … no one knew where he was and … couldn't get it … it was the only copy I had … I was going to make a book of it … T'was only thirty-six foolscap pages. I had tons more stuff to put into it but I couldn't fit it in, I left it too late. There's a lot of things I was going to fill in again, after.

Once Mulvihill had finally retrieved his manuscript from Casey, but having failed to have the memoir published in the 1980s, a handful of copies were given to neighbours, family and old comrades. One of the very few surviving copies included a title written in his own hand at the top of the opening page – *One Man's Ireland*. I first obtained a copy when I was researching the Ballymacandy ambush in 2020–21; it was provided by the family of the late Paul Lucey, whose father, Con, was the commanding officer of the IRA in Caragh Lake, south of Killorglin, and alongside whom Dan Mulvihill plotted and carried out many attacks on the enemy.[6] The memoir greatly enhanced the telling of the ambush story. A stage dramatisation of *Ballymacandy* encouraged not only a newfound appreciation in his own community of the role that Mulvihill played in the revolutionary years but also prompted a deeper exploration by this author of his motivations, his influences, his ambitions and his legacy. And thus, forty years after his death, Mulvihill's ambition that his memoir be published is fulfilled.

The memoir, which forms the backbone of this book, is a rich and valuable account of life in Kerry and in Ireland throughout the twentieth century. First-hand accounts of the revolutionary years in Ireland, from the Easter Rising of 1916 to the War of Independence and the Civil War which followed, remain a rarity. In Kerry, only a very small number of Mulvihill's contemporaries penned their recollections of the period. Billy Mullins of Moyderwell, Tralee, published his memoir in 1983: it covers the entirety of the revolutionary period from before the Easter Rising to the end of the Civil War and, very valuably from a historical perspective, is replete with a large number of images from the period.[7] A chance search of an attic in Pennsylvania in 1990 brought another such testimony to light: the memoir of Jeremiah Murphy, *When Youth Was Mine*, an account of the wars in east Kerry.[8] Another well-known memoir is that of the Knocknagoshel schoolteacher Seamus O'Connor, who provides a social as well as political and military record of events.[9]

Mulvihill's reminiscences stand out from this existing corpus of memoirs in several ways and, as such, represent a distinctive and significant contribution to the historiography. Not only does his memoir document the writer's early years and the evolution of his political outlook, but it also charts his life and times after the revolution and, unlike many of his contemporaries who played no further role in the IRA or in political life, it details how Mulvihill continued to be very active and involved in republicanism, particularly in the years before the Second World War. It also illuminates the challenges which the veterans of the revolution – men and women –

faced as they battled for paltry pension payments, as well as acknowledgement by and recognition from the Irish state. Critically too, it offers insights into the mindset of a republican reflecting on the developments in Northern Ireland and the Troubles – and the continuum of the conflict of the 1920s – as his life comes to an end. Ultimately, it is about one man's Ireland, an Ireland which Dan Mulvihill tried to shape and influence in his own way and who, thankfully, recorded the many dramatic twists and turns in his life as an Irish republican.

CHAPTER 1

'Great fighters and men of splendid physique'

GEARÓID MULVIHILL WAS ONE of Dan Mulvihill's better-known ancestors. A descendant of the Mulvihills of Knockanira in rural County Clare, a family known for 'great fighters and men of splendid physique', Gearóid was among the best faction fighters of his generation and a leader of men in his native north Kerry.[1] He had a habit of stuffing hay into his cap to cushion blows to the head during the fighting. A wallop from a blackthorn stick or a crudely fashioned cudgel left many a man bleeding profusely, prostrate on the ground for hours; it left others dead. Anything that might lessen the impact was a bonus.

The practice of faction fighting between rival families and their allies was a controversial but common feature of late-nineteenth-century life in rural Ireland and sometimes involved hundreds or even thousands of men and women engaged in beating each other with sticks and a variety of improvised weapons.[2] Often rooted in personal and familial rivalries and animosities, part territorialism, part pastime, the practice became particularly prevalent in rural Kerry in the mid-1800s, especially in north Kerry, in parishes like Ballyduff, Ballylongford, Ardfert and Ballyheigue.[3]

Gearóid Mulvihill was one of Kerry's best-known and most ruthless faction fighters. He had a reputation as an intimidating foe. In his survey of faction fighting in Kerry in the 1800s, Seán Moraghan provides a description of the 'formidable' Mulvihill:

> Gearóid Mulvihill had many notable victories and was held in high esteem even by his enemies. At that time the champions' different factions used to challenge each other to fight in order to see who was the better man ... Big Jim Hartnett of Abbeyfeale sent a challenge to Gearóid which he accepted. He took none of his followers with him. It was a long hard fight which Gearóid eventually won.[4]

Gearóid was a member of the so-called 'Black Mulvihills' of north Kerry, who developed a reputation as a fearsome and fearless gang. The origins of the 'Black' epithet were never clearly explained but it was a feature of Irish surname etymology for generations. From the ancient Irish barony of Iraghticonnor, the extended family resided in the part of north Kerry that includes the large market town of Listowel and its hinterland and stretched northwards to the Shannon estuary. In the nineteenth century the area was also home to two other well-known factions, the Lawlors and the Cooleens.

The Cooleens and the Mulvihills had a particularly bitter and bloody rivalry. At the so-called Battle of Ballyeagh near Ballybunion on 24 June 1834, they took part in the most notorious fight of the period, which 'left between eighteen and twenty-nine people dead, scandalised the local and national press, required two official inquiries, and resulted in transportation for a number of north Kerry men'.[5] Described as 'murderous carnage' by *The Kerry Evening Post*, the battle involved the use of sticks, hurleys and stones, which were used by women as well as men:

> Up to Monday, the bodies of sixteen men had been found, and so dreadfully mutilated on both head and arms as fully to bear out the horrifying evidence which appeared before several inquests held on the bodies, and it appears that immediately on the party being pursued being upset in the water, their merciless pursuers waded in after them, some on foot and others on horseback, and on the persons upset raising their heads above the water, these wretches [women] commenced cleaving them with hurleys, sticks, and stones ...[6]

As a young man, Dan Mulvihill would often be reminded of his ancestry by his mother. Hanoria (Nora) Mulvihill was actually descended from the Cooleens, but love appears to have transcended any remaining inter-family rivalries when she met and married Cornelius Mulvihill. During an encounter in Dingle many years later, in 1922, Dan was again reminded of his forefathers. He was in west Kerry due to his role as the liaison officer for County Kerry, to which he was appointed following the end of the War of Independence:

> We went into Benner's Hotel [Dingle] and we were not long there when someone introduced us to the tall local curate, Father Finucane. He heard my name looking at me and said – 'Holy God, another Black Mulvihill.' I had spent the years of my childhood listening to that. My mother was a 'Cooleen', and my grandfather was a Black Mulvihill, so I knew what he was talking about. My grandfather had been born a few years after the fight, my mother in the [18]60s.

Family lore retained its own version of the Battle of Ballyeagh, as Mulvihill later wrote:

> Their telling of the fight – and they both agreed – was that the Cooleens won. The fight started with an argument between two men, one from each side going to a fair in Tralee, in early Spring, and it gradually built up to the meeting in Ballyeagh. Their telling of it was that the Mulvihill/Lawlor crowd beat the other crowd back across the river and followed them. The Cooleen women, who were waiting for their men, saw what was happening,

> took off their black stockings and loaded them to the heel with sand and gravel, and as the Black Mulvihill faction arrived, they bashed their heads and let them go with the tide. I think there were over twenty drowned.

At some point in the late 1800s, Dan Mulvihill's grandfather, James, moved to and settled on a farm near the village of Castlemaine in mid-Kerry, south of the bailiwick of his Black Mulvihill clan. James farmed land on the banks of the River Maine in the townland of Brackhill (or *Cnoc Breac* in Irish, translating as speckled hill). He had been born a decade before the Great Hunger, which forced many off their land through eviction or starvation and which may have accounted for him settling at Brackhill. It was fertile and arable land, and by the beginning of the twentieth century, the family were 'fairly average size farmers' with 120 acres.[7] Compared to many of their neighbours, it was a relatively large farm holding on which there were six outhouses and sheds.[8] The Mulvihill family lived in a large farmhouse, which, at the beginning of the twentieth century, was home to James and his wife, Bridget, as well as Dan's parents, Cornelius and Nora, and their six children: four sons, Matthew, Patrick, Daniel and Timothy (known as 'Todd'), and two daughters, Bridget and Katie.[9] Another daughter, unnamed, 'died as a child'.[10] The family had a live-in servant, Margaret Clifford, to assist with raising the family and running the household.

It was at Brackhill that Dan Mulvihill was born in 1897. His mother was and would remain a particular influence on the young Mulvihill, personally and politically. 'She knew more about Irish history than anyone I have ever met since,' he recalled, adding 'my mother was one of the greatest Irishwomen I ever knew'.[11] Nora was fond of sharing stories of the Fenians, the Irish republican group who led a campaign against British rule in the middle of the nineteenth century. One of its most prominent leaders, Jeremiah O'Donovan Rossa, had a close connection with Milltown – a village two miles from the Mulvihill farm – as Nora would recount: Rossa had married Nano Eager from the village in 1853.[12] Nora also recalled having listened to the speeches of another Fenian with Milltown connections, Jeremiah D. Sheehan, who was later a Member of Parliament (MP) for Kerry.

As a boy Mulvihill would have attended the local national school and helped out on the farm, but when the outbreak of the First World War in 1914 brought increased political instability and economic upheaval in Ireland, employment prospects became scarce and so he decided to train as a telegraphist. A relation of the Mulvihill family worked at the Western College of Telegraphy in Kilrush in County Clare:

> In 1915, I went to [a] school in Kilrush run by a cousin of mine. There, I learned the Morse Code so as to get into Marconi House [in London] as a Learner. You had to be able to send and receive eighteen words per minute. That was my first time leaving home[,] in the summer of 1915. West Clare people were the nicest I ever met.

Just as the Easter Rising – in which members of the Irish Volunteers, the Irish Citizen Army and the Irish Republican Brotherhood (IRB) staged a week-long rebellion against British rule – got underway in the capital, Mulvihill was leaving the country:

> I went to London in April 1916, stood the test, and was admitted [to Marconi House] as a Learner at 17/6p per week. I paid 15/– per week for digs in Praed St. just across from St. Mary's Hospital. We were trained in the underground portion of Marconi House as we were [for] the Air Corps and Marines. All had different classes, but we all mixed during off hours and struck up some rare friendships.

Marconi House was the headquarters of the Wireless Telegraph and Signal Company (later known as the Marconi Company), which was founded by the Italian engineer and Nobel Prize winner Guglielmo Marconi. The aristocrat is credited with the invention of radio and the use of radio-based wireless telegraphy. The large eight-storey building at 335 The Strand, where the teenage Mulvihill arrived in the spring of 1916, dominated the junction of Strand and Aldwych and had originally been a hotel and restaurant adjacent to the Gaiety Theatre. Marconi House provided training as well as employment, and Mulvihill initially attended evening classes to become more proficient at Morse Code:

> We worked from seven to nine three evenings a week. There were eight classes there, an exam at the end of

> weeks, and if you got through that, you were admitted into the next class. I went straight through the eight, and in the exam in August [1916], I got a first-class P.Y.G. This meant that you were able to send and receive at twenty-five words per minute, and that you could take the [wireless] set asunder and assemble it again. The set took up half a room at that time. You could put one of the same power in a very small space now.

Mulvihill's innate interest in international events and the history of other parts of the world was apparent in his late teens and he recalls some of the major incidents of the First World War: 'I was working in Marconi House the night the account arrived that the cruiser on which Kitchener was going to Russia had been torpedoed.[13] There were all sorts of yarns about it at the time, even in Marconi House. I took no notice. I did not even know that he was a Kerryman.'

It wasn't all work and no play for the young Mulvihill in London, though:

> We had a lot of spare time, and I spent a good part of it in Hyde Park, pulling a boat up and down the Serpentine, when I had the money.[14] I think it was sixpence an hour, and otherwise lying under a tree reading science fiction. Believe it or not, there was a lot of it being published at the time, such as H.G. Wells, Jules Verne, Rider Haggard, Griffith etc. I enjoyed London while I was there and thought there was more freedom there than any place I

> ever went afterwards. I still think that in their own land, the British are outstanding in the world.
>
> I met a fellow from Canada: a ginger-head and we used to go to a place called Hendon (Stagg Lane). I went flying with him there, in a bi-plane, a far reach from today – they were all wicker work, plywood and canvas – but could fly from fifty to eighty miles per hour. I wanted to join the Air Corps but would not be released [from training]. I worked like a devil there as it was something I was interested in.

Mulvihill's aspiration to join the British Air Force suggests not only a youthful exuberance and sense of adventure but also proves that he had no apparent political allegiances or strongly held views in his late teens and early twenties. Nor is there any evidence that he was involved in the many Irish political and cultural organisations in London at this time. Many of those with whom Mulvihill would later fight against the Crown forces in his native county cut their political teeth in London in the years before the Easter Rising of 1916. Denis Daly from Cahersiveen – later a prominent anti-Treaty IRA member and a Fianna Fáil Teachta Dála (TD) for Kerry – was employed in London before the Rising and joined the IRB in the city in 1913 before he returned to participate in the rebellion.[15] Another south Kerry man, Con Keating, who drowned at Ballykissane Pier near Killorglin on the eve of the Rising, studied wireless telegraphy and was also active in the IRB in London.[16] However, by the time Dan Mulvihill arrived in the English capital in April

1916, men like Daly and Keating had returned to Ireland and the Rising was over.

The rebellion of 1916 had claimed the life of a cousin of Mulvihill. Michael Mulvihill of Ardoughter, Ballyduff, was one of four Kerry men killed in the fighting in Dublin during Easter Week. He died on Moore Lane on 28 April, in the same hail of gunfire which claimed the lives of fellow Kerry natives Michael Joseph O'Rahilly ('The O'Rahilly') from Ballylongford, Patrick Shortis of Ballybunion and Patrick O'Connor of Rathmore.[17] Dan Mulvihill likely learned of his cousin's fate while he was in London. During the trial of Roger Casement in that city in the summer of 1916, Mulvihill recalled seeing the prisoner 'being taken into Bow Street' magistrates' court one day and how he detested seeing the uniforms of the Royal Irish Constabulary (RIC) who were present for the arraignment.[18] Though there is no evidence that Mulvihill considered joining the many Irish republican groups in London, he must have been moved by the death of his cousin as well as the trial and execution of Casement, which provoked widespread revulsion.

As he turned twenty years of age, Mulvihill appeared to be more interested in enjoying city life while he had the opportunity. Apart from idling around Hyde Park and indulging his new interest in flying, Mulvihill developed another lifelong passion while he lived in London. Throughout his life, he was an avid film buff and, in later life, he collected and shared with friends many movies, particularly Westerns. This appetite was whetted in London:

> I loved films and they were in their infancy then. I enjoyed Charlie Chaplin, *The Keystone Cops*, *The Exploits of Elaine*.[19] I often went to two different houses [cinemas] in the same night. It cost twopence 'in the Gods' but with free passes, I got to a lot of the theatres, and as far as possible wandered around on foot, over most of the West End, and usually walked from Strand to Praed St., coming up through Soho, back by Regent's Park, Baker Street and out at the junction of Edgeware Road and Harrow Road. Around Marble Arch was a lovely spot in the month of June.

The relaxation and exploits of the summer quickly came to a halt when Mulvihill was called to Liverpool to take up a position with Alfred Booth and Company (better known as the Booth Line), a large merchant shipping company based in the city. He was offered a telegraphy post on the SS *Aidan*, a sizeable passenger ship that was first launched in 1911 and accommodated 146 passengers. The SS *Aidan* departed from Liverpool docks on 11 August 1916 with Mulvihill on board. The date was one that he easily remembered: 11 August was and remains the second day of the annual Puck Fair festival in Killorglin, just a few miles from Mulvihill's home at Brackhill. The trip took him to Central and South America:

> We were bound for the Gulf of Mexico and after getting over the seasickness, I liked the wandering from port to port. There were two radio operators on board, six

> hours on and six hours off, and the grub was the best I have ever eaten, though I have stayed in the best hotels since in about ten countries. None of them could touch the Officers' Mess of any ship I was ever on. On that first trip we went to about six different ports, the first was Galveston, the second Corpus Christi and, I think, Havana. I would get mixed up if I tried to sort them all out. From Maine to Buenos Aires, Montevideo, Rio [de Janeiro], up the Amazon, down the Mediterranean. The pay was no good, but there was plenty of idle time. When a ship came inside the five-mile limit, the Wireless Cabin was sealed, and we were off until she cleared it again.

During part of his trip, outside Havana, the SS *Aidan* was struck by 'a cyclone' and it finished up 'near the coast of Maine'. Overall, his experience was hugely positive, however: there were 'a lot of beautiful places,' Mulvihill recalled.[20]

+++

During Mulvihill's teenage years and while he was in London, political developments in his native parish and his native county had moved apace. Companies of the Irish Volunteers were established across Kerry following the foundation of the organisation in November 1913 in Dublin. Set up in opposition to the formation of the Ulster Volunteers, who vehemently opposed Home Rule for Ireland, the Irish Volunteers aimed to 'secure and maintain the rights and liberties common to the whole people of Ireland' and had some 200,000 members within a year of its launch. Five months after the foundation of the Irish Volunteers in Dublin, a company was established in Milltown in March 1914, one of the first in Kerry. Evidence for Volunteer activity in the village at this time comes from a report in the *Killarney Echo and South Kerry Chronicle* on 28 March 1914: 'I am also informed that at 4 p.m. on the same date and place the Milltown and Parish Volunteer Force will be organized. All the young blood and the old veterans are expected to attend. Drill instructors will be present. Up Kerry!'

The following month, the Milltown Volunteers had, according to the *Kerry Weekly Reporter*, a 'very interesting march':

> By arrangement, upwards of 100 members, principally members of the Ancient Order of Hibernians, met the Killorglin volunteers headed up by the splendid Brass Band of the Young Men's Total Abstinence Society at a place called Turnhally [Tinahally], midway between Killorglin and Milltown. Both companies marched into Killorglin and formed in the Square. Having gone through their drill by instructors O'Shea and Flynn, the Milltown Volunteers returned to Milltown.[21]

Against this backdrop, the local MP, Thomas O'Donnell, spoke at public meetings in Milltown about the need for Home Rule for Ireland to wipe away 'the stain of slavery under which we had lived for so long'.[22] Speeches were often preceded by a parade of Volunteers and a marching band.

At the same time, tenant agitation was adding an edge to local politics. The local Tenants' Association, established in 1913, aimed to achieve 'the improvement of our homes and to try and reduce the over-taxed rents we are trying to meet'.[23] With the support of the wider farming community, the group pledged to withdraw rents from the local landlords, the Godfrey family, 'until our houses are put in proper sanitary condition'. They also called on the Congested Districts Board to 'divide Lyre farm amongst the people of the town', a call for which they sought the support of the local parish priest, Fr Patrick Buckley, and the Bishop of Kerry, John Mangan. Resolutions of the association, meetings of which were often attended by Rural District Council members A.W. Murphy and Michael Heffernan, were often sent to the leader of the Irish Parliamentary Party, John Redmond, as well as Kerry MPs.[24]

A native of Milltown was among those who took part in the Easter Rising in 1916: Philip (Phil) Joseph McMahon was born in 1888 and grew up at Main Street, where his father, Bernard, was an RIC officer. He moved to Ardee in County Louth and joined the local company of the Irish Volunteers. McMahon was arrested for seizing rifles and ammunition, jailed and later sentenced to death (commuted).[25] During 1916, however, there is little evidence of activity on behalf of the Volunteers in Milltown. That was all about to change.

+++

Dan Mulvihill returned from his posting with the SS *Aidan* towards the end of 1916. The reasons for his return home aren't specified in his memoir or other accounts: perhaps the job was temporary or he may have been made redundant, but he found himself at home at Brackhill in the early winter. In the preceding months, political sentiment had shifted considerably. Initially, many Irish people had been sceptical of, if not hostile to, the actions of those who had instigated and participated in the Easter Rising in April 1916. For example, a meeting of Kerry County Council was told the rebellion was nothing but a 'criminal folly in Dublin'.[26] However, the way in which the rebel leaders were summarily tried and executed caused outrage, and the hanging of Roger Casement for treason in August infuriated even those without any strong anti-British feelings. The reprisal killings were a boon to the republican party, Sinn Féin, and the Volunteers. In Kerry, and across the country, the Volunteers and Cumann na mBan began to reorganise, and their ranks grew in number; within a year of the Rising there were an estimated 3,000 Volunteers in Kerry, increasing from just several hundred before the rebellion.[27]

In November 1916 the local branch of Sinn Féin arranged a meeting in Milltown. The only item on the agenda was a coming together of the party and the local branch of the Volunteers. Mulvihill was among those who attended:

> This was a changing over of the Sinn Féin club to a Volunteer Company. Tom [O']Connor, Knokreagh [Knockreigh], became O/C [Officer Commanding]. There would have

> been about thirty or forty of us there that night ... the average of the fellows would have been sixteen to twenty, with six or seven older men who were the Sinn Féin Club. Tom [O']Neill, carpenter, was the man who suggested the change; he was in charge of the Sinn Féin Club and would have been about forty years [old] at that time. He joined the Volunteers and served until the start of the Civil War.[28]

Callinafercy, a large townland between Killorglin and Milltown, established its own company in the spring of 1917. A company was also formed in Kiltallagh, which encompassed much of the greater Castlemaine area, but Mulvihill remained with the Milltown Company, most likely because his home was within the boundary of Milltown parish.

It wasn't just the menfolk who were organising. Large numbers of women, many of them sisters and relatives of the Volunteers, joined the new women's organisation, Cumann na mBan. Founded in 1914 at Wynn's Hotel in Dublin, Cumann na mBan aimed to 'provide a platform from which nationalist women could work for the cause of Ireland'.[29] The Milltown District Council of Cumann na mBan was part of A Company of the 6th Battalion of the 2nd Kerry Brigade in the Southern Division. It was formed in 1918 under the captaincy of May Allman, sister of Daniel Allman of Rockfield, who would be killed at the Headford Junction ambush in 1921. Katie Mulvihill and her sister, Bridget (Bridie), were among the first to join the Milltown Cumann na mBan.[30] In subsequent years, Katie 'carried dispatches' and 'provided food and sleeping accommodation' for many IRA men who were on the run.[31] Their neighbour at Brackhill, Annie Cronin, was another recruit. Like the Mulvihills, Cronin, born in 1901, came from a family immersed in the republican movement. Each of her brothers joined the IRA and Jimmy, in particular, was one of Dan Mulvihill's closest allies. Annie Cronin's pension application records that she was treasurer of the local branch and attended first aid classes 'conducted by Dr Sheehan, Milltown', who acted as medical officer to the local IRA during the War of Independence.

Mulvihill and the local IRA organised and trained throughout 1917 and 1918: 'During the following couple of years it was just routine. I know that at the time of the "German Plot" nine or ten of us used to go off drilling on Saturday. This continued up to 1919.'[32] The German Plot was a conspiracy advanced by the British that Sinn Féin was plotting with Germany to stage a rebellion in Ireland, which they used to intern Irish Volunteers without trial. Several of Mulvihill's contemporaries, among them Thomas O'Connor of Milltown, were jailed on trumped-up charges, and they refused to recognise the court when arraigned. O'Connor recalled that so appalling and traumatic were the conditions in jail that 'one or two of the lads were removed to the Mental Hospital'.[33]

The months after the end of the First World War were bleak. Mulvihill found himself at 'a dead end' and he went to 'winter classes' in 1918–19 in nearby Castlemaine to pass the time. His older brother, Patrick, a qualified doctor, encouraged him to pursue a proper education. Within a few weeks, and with the encouragement of his family, he secured a scholarship to allow him to take up a place at the agricultural college in Clonakilty in County Cork:

> I think now that I was fairly wild, but it was a great place and we had lots of time off for playing games. I played both hurling and football: hurling came first. Three of us, who had no money for a football, made hurleys of our own, more like bats, and played with a half solid ball that was used for handball. I was well away there, as house master J. Hassett, from Clare, who was a friend of my brother's, was a member of the Cork hurling team.[34] They had played together at U.C.C. We had some great hurlers in Clon that year from Cork, Limerick, Kilkenny, Tipperary, and Wexford.

Mulvihill's arrival in west Cork at the beginning of 1919 coincided with a time of extraordinary political turmoil in Ireland. On 21 January a group of Sinn Féin politicians who had been elected MPs in the British general election the previous month assembled at the Mansion House in Dublin to establish their own independent parliament, Dáil Éireann. Though many of its members were in jail at the behest of the British authorities – just one of Kerry's four TDs, Piaras Béaslaí, was present – the new assembly declared itself the only legitimate parliament of the Irish Republic. On the same day, the first of many engagements of what became known as the War of Independence occurred in Soloheadbeg in County

Tipperary, when two policemen were killed in an ambush by Irish Volunteers.

Mulvihill had just moved to an area of the country in which the War of Independence would be fought with a ferocity and intensity unequalled in many other parts of Ireland. It was in Clonakilty in the early months of 1919 that he first cut his political and paramilitary teeth under the influence of senior and significant figures in the conflict and in an area that would be a hotbed of violence and disruption during the fight against the forces of the Crown. Between 1919 and 1921 'Rebel Cork' was 'the most violent county in Ireland'[35] and Mulvihill adored his time there:

> My chief *grá* [love] for west Cork was that it was a great I.R.A. centre. Greatest in Ireland at the time. There was a world of great men there. I'll only mention for [*sic*] ones I knew well. They were all [Flying] Column men later, Stephen O'Neill,[36] Spud Murphy,[37] 'Flier' Nyhan,[38] and my greatest friend, Jim Hurley. I used to play mid-field on Jim, but outside of that we had a lot of other things in common.

Clonakilty native Jim Hurley played a prominent role in the Cork No. 3 Brigade, which included Bandon, Bantry, Skibbereen and Castletownbere. Hurley was a member of the ambush party that launched the attack at Béal na Bláth on 22 August 1922 in which Michael Collins was killed. He was perhaps better-known as a player of inter-county football and hurling with Cork, winning four All-Ireland hurling medals. In Hurley, Mulvihill found not only someone who shared his love of Gaelic games but who also tutored and mentored him politically.

Though already a member of the Volunteers in his native Kerry, Mulvihill threw his weight behind the activities of the Volunteers in west Cork. It was in this period that Mulvihill first encountered the enemy:

> ... the British were in the workhouse at the Bandon Cross Junction of the road as we went into town. Our half day was Saturday, and we always went to town. Out in March [1919] the trouble started, and it gradually grew worse.[39] Sometime towards the end of June, there was one hell of a row fighting with soldiers and we were banned from going to town. We went anyway and two Kerry fellows were sacked.[40] Two-thirds of the fellows walked out with them. I hated to leave as Clon[akilty] held the finest fellows and girls in the south at the time.

With his first taste of interaction with the Crown forces under his belt, Mulvihill returned to Brackhill. As Christmas 1919 approached, tragedy struck when his brother, Patrick, succumbed to tuberculosis. The return to Brackhill meant not only a period of mourning for Dan Mulvihill but also a period of growing politicisation of the young Kerryman and an increasing involvement in Irish republicanism.

CHAPTER 2

'Calm before the storm'

FRESH FROM HIS INVOLVEMENT with the Volunteers of west Cork and a skirmish with the Crown forces, Mulvihill quickly rejoined the ranks of the organisation – which in 1920, adopted the name of Irish Republican Army – in his home place. Many of his nearest neighbours in Brackhill, such as Denis Dowd, Jack Flynn and Jimmy Cronin, had joined the Milltown IRA, and at the beginning of 1920, Mulvihill, in his own words, 'fell in with the [IRA] Company'. 'There was a lull,' he remembered, a 'calm before the storm, everyone waiting'. The lull to which Mulvihill referred – in the earlier months of the 1920s – was a period of relative calm in Kerry despite the ongoing war. This allowed the IRA to organise and mobilise and to develop a relatively sophisticated organisational structure and disciplinary line of command. County Kerry was divided into three brigade areas: Kerry No. 1 Brigade, including north and west Kerry with the county town, Tralee, at its centre; Kerry No. 2 Brigade, covering east Kerry, much of mid-Kerry as well as Killarney and Kenmare;

and Kerry No. 3 Brigade, which was based in the southern half of the Iveragh Peninsula and included Cahersiveen.

Mulvihill and his comrades were part of the 6th Battalion of the Kerry No. 2 Brigade. The battalion included the IRA companies from Killorglin, Glenbeigh, Kilgobnet, Caragh Lake and Mulvihill's company in Milltown.[1] Mulvihill's neighbour and fellow Volunteer Jimmy Cronin described the situation locally at the beginning of 1920:

> In January, 1920, things were very quiet in our Battalion area and in order to get things going some of us decided to go 'on the run'. I went with Dan Mulvihill and Jack Flynn (T.D.) of Milltown Company and we were joined by Batty Dwyer, Paddy (Rua) O'Sullivan, Seamus Mahony and Martin Wade of the Killorglin Company. Thomas O'Connor, who was Battalion O/C came with us. We made our headquarters at Glencar which is about 18 miles back into the mountains to the south of the Killorglin–Caherciveen Road. We remained there a short time and we then received a message from P.J. Cahill, Officer Commanding Kerry No. 1. Brigade. He asked that myself, Dan Mulvihill, Jack Flynn (T.D.) and Thomas O'Connor should join Kerry No. 1. Flying Column.[2]

The 'flying column' was an effective weapon used by the IRA to target the enemy. The best fighters were chosen to launch surprise attacks on the Crown forces and then withdraw from the scene very quickly before returning to a safe house or hideout. From Glencar, a handful of attacks on the Crown forces were launched, including an audacious assault on the headquarters of the police force, the RIC, in Killorglin in the spring of 1920:

> We took about 30 men into Killorglin that night. We were joined near the town by the main body of the column. Bunches of men occupied houses in different positions and we moved into a position at the Ball Alley at the top of the town. We hit up a patrol which was returning to barracks. A general shoot up followed for half an hour or more after which we retreated.[3]

As the conflict in Kerry and elsewhere settled into something of a stalemate in the spring of 1920, the British government recognised the need for additional manpower to take the fight to the IRA. It was increasingly realised that the RIC was simply 'not up to the job'.[4] Critically, from a policing and security perspective, the force was neither experienced enough nor equipped to deal with an insurgency.

The arrival of the Black and Tans – so-called because of the colour of their uniforms – in the middle of 1920 added a new intensity and ferocity to the war. They were a supplementary force sent to Ireland to assist the RIC in suppressing IRA violence. Made up primarily of veterans of the First World War, many of whom had experienced the horrors of the trenches along the Western Front, the force had a reputation for indiscriminate violence and indiscipline, which made it synonymous with the most controversial episodes of the War of Independence. The RIC was further supplemented by a second military unit of about 8,000 men, the Auxiliary Division – dubbed the 'Auxies' by the IRA.

The summer of 1920 witnessed a rapid intensification of fighting and savagery in Kerry with an increase in ambushes, killings and assaults. It was not long before Mulvihill became immersed in the type of ambushes on police and army for which the IRA was renowned. The ambush had become the IRA modus operandi extraordinaire. Using the intelligence gathered by IRA scouts and members of Cumann na mBan, who familiarised themselves with the movements of the various units of the Crown forces, and capitalising on a superior knowledge of the terrain and the roads in rural areas, it became a successful tool in the IRA's military strategy. A target or targets would be chosen, they would be closely observed for days or perhaps weeks, a location would be chosen and IRA men would assemble and lie in wait. Invariably launched from higher ground or sheltered areas, those being attacked were left with little or no cover or escape from the hail of fire that would rain down on them. The assailants would then disperse promptly in multiple directions to their network of safe houses or rural dugouts, thereby – usually – evading capture.

A bold attempt to ambush a patrol of Black and Tans near the main road between Killorglin and Killarney was one such example; it was an attack in which Mulvihill was central to the planning and initiation. On 16 August 1920 several IRA companies in mid-Kerry prepared for the ambush as their targets travelled along the main road at Beaufort. Among those involved with Mulvihill were Daniel and Pat Allman of the nearby Listry IRA, Jimmy Cronin of the Milltown IRA, Tommy Woods and brothers Batt and Patrick Riordan of the Firies Company, as well as the Dálaigh brothers of Knockaneacoolteen, Tom and Charlie.[5] The ambush, however, did not go precisely to plan, as Mulvihill recounted:

> The position for ambush was on an old road west of Beaufort, nearly facing the main road with a good fall.[6] A horse cart had been backed up the slope and was held in position by [an IRA] man with a rope. When he would get [the] signal, the rope would be released, and the cart would run forward and block the road. It was a private car with some [Black and Tan] officers that came [from Killarney], and when the signal was given and the rope was released, the cart only went forward about two feet and stopped. The Tan car sped on though a couple of shots were fired at it. Just before this happened, I watched a number of fellows and girls on horseback come along and turn up the bridge to Beaufort. They were gone to the end of the bridge when the car came along.

By an extraordinary coincidence, among the 'fellows and girls on horseback' was the American writer, journalist and adventurer Negley Farson and his wife, Enid Eveleen (née Stoker), a niece of the author of *Dracula*, Bram Stoker. The couple had been staying at Flesk Castle in Killarney and were on their way to 'The Reeks' in Beaufort. The large period house was the home of the Gaelic chieftain, the McGillycuddy of the Reeks. The McGillycuddy, Ross Kinloch McGillycuddy, was later a member of the Irish Senate. His mother, Agnes, was married to Enid's uncle, Dr George Stoker. A quarter of a century later, Farson recounted his encounter with the IRA in his autobiography: 'We went up on horseback through the Gap of Dunloe – riding within three yards of a Sinn Féin ambush that an hour later bushwhacked some British officers.'[7]

Mulvihill happened across Farson's account in his book many years later:

> Twenty-five years later when reading Negley Farson's book, *The Way of a Transgressor*, I came across mention of the ambush.[8] He had been one of the crowd on horseback that day. They had come from Flesk Castle, with him was the girl he later married, daughter or niece of Bram Stoker. I had read *Dracula* and liked it, it was years later before it became famous, but Farson's book is far ahead of it.

+++

By the summer of 1920 the war in Kerry had settled into a steady pattern of IRA ambushes and retaliatory attacks by the Crown forces on IRA volunteers' homes and the civilian population. Increasingly, the focus of Mulvihill and his comrades turned to the barracks in which the RIC, as well as many members of the Auxiliaries and the Black and Tans, were based. Barracks was often a misnomer – in very rural areas, police were often based in nothing more than rudimentary huts, which offered little or no protection. By virtue of their location in rural and isolated areas, barracks were vulnerable to attack. Crucially, they provided a source of weapons and ammunition for IRA volunteers, and raids upon barracks or their destruction, often by arson, represented a body-blow to British power in Ireland.

During the early months of 1920, there was a series of attacks on barracks in Kerry, including at Camp, Ballybunion, Gortatlea and Scartaglen. Several other abandoned police posts were burned down, including at Templenoe, Headford, Ballyheigue and Ardfert.[9] Between 1919 and 1921, there were 267 incidents of damage to police barracks in Ireland and twenty-five were completely destroyed.[10] By the end of the war, over thirty barracks in Kerry had been shut down or abandoned.[11]

Two such barracks within Mulvihill's brigade area, which the RIC were forced to abandon in 1920, were outposts in Boolteens, a few miles from his home, and Glencar, a sprawling rural and sparsely populated parish south of Killorglin. In Glencar, the RIC abandoned their post in June following an IRA ambush of a local police patrol and the area became, in Mulvihill's own words, 'a small Republic'. When the RIC in Milltown relocated their barracks to another part of the village, the former barracks was attacked by Mulvihill and the Milltown IRA in an attempt to prevent their return there and to send a signal to the local Crown forces: 'The R.I.C. vacated Milltown barracks, and we tried to make it uninhabitable.[12] We made a bad job of it as we had no explosives and burning [it] meant burning other houses.'

The failure to destroy the vacated premises was at least partially owing to the need to avoid civilian casualties and damage to shops and businesses located adjacent to the barracks. The IRA relied heavily on the support, or at least the passivity, of the civilian population in villages like Milltown, and any damage to property or impact on commercial activity would have alienated a population already suffering under the manifold consequences of the ongoing war.

One of those consequences was the effect on communication and on postal services in particular. A much-favoured tactic of the IRA was holding up and raiding trains with a view to intercepting communications between the Crown forces in different parts of the country. Moreover, the interference with rail services, which sometimes involved the removal of railway tracks or the blowing up of lines, disrupted the movement or transportation of troops. Mulvihill and his men took part in many such activities: 'Sometime about the 16th September [1920] we held up the mail train at Castlemaine, took the mails for the area, censored them and returned them a few nights later.'[13]

+++

The end of October and the beginning of November 1920 brought about an intensification of hostilities in the county and in mid-Kerry in particular, which brought Mulvihill into much closer contact – and much greater danger – in his engagements with the RIC and the other divisions of the Crown forces. Events in other parts of the country conspired to create a heightened tension and a vicious escalation in violence. The death of the Sinn Féin lord mayor of Cork after seventy-four days on hunger strike on 25 October 1920 triggered significant consequences for the IRA in Kerry and beyond. Terence MacSwiney, who had been jailed on charges of sedition and denied release despite his elected office, became a martyr, and his death was the subject of international headlines. A week later, on 1 November, eighteen-year-old medical student Kevin Barry was hanged for his role in an attack on British forces. These deaths infused the war with a new bile and generated vicious retaliatory attacks by the IRA across the country. Mulvihill was not exaggerating when he recalled that, in the week of the two high-profile deaths, 'things started to get rough'. Reprisals and counter-reprisals increased in number and intensity:

> Things started to get rough: Terence MacSwiney was slowly dying in an English Prison. We tried twice to get a shot at Auxiliaries who visited the area, but we always failed, as they never went the same way twice. Terence MacSwiney died in Brixton, and Paddy Cahill, Brigade O/C Kerry No. 1, issued a brigade order that any member of British Forces, wherever found, in or out of uniform, on the night of 31st October [1920], was to be executed.[14]

> This order was carried out. I don't think an order like this was issued by any other Brigade ... on [1] November morning from Tarbert to Killorglin, fires were blazing as the [Black and] Tans ran amok ... Tralee town was closed down on a 24-hour curfew. The army had promised to guard the town. They went back to [the] Barracks at midnight and the Tans came out and started to burn and wreck. They put sentries on bakeries and provision stores. This continued for days.

The protracted shutdown of Tralee to which Mulvihill refers became known as the Siege of Tralee and lasted for nine days. It was prompted by the IRA murder of two RIC constables, Ernest Bright and Patrick Waters, killings which were considered reprisals for the death of Terence MacSwiney. The Black and Tans imposed a strict curfew in the town, ordered all local shops and businesses to shut their doors, and prevented goods and foodstuffs from entering Tralee. Amid the tensions, two local civilians, Thomas Wall and John Conway, were shot dead before the Chief Secretary for Ireland, Hamar Greenwood, finally ordered the lifting of the siege on 9 November.

The beginning of the Siege of Tralee coincided with rising tensions in mid-Kerry and events that propelled Dan Mulvihill to the centre of combat with the Black and Tans. At about 10 p.m. on 31 October, members of the IRA confronted two Black and Tans at Hillville, on the Milltown to Killorglin road. Twenty-year old Constable John Herbert Evans, a former First World War Royal Air Force pilot, and twenty-four-year-old Constable

Albert Caseley from London were both off duty for the evening and had been seeing two local girls – a practice which was often dubbed 'company keeping' and was much frowned upon by the IRA. The men who were lying in wait at Hillville were acting on intelligence gathered by the local members of Cumann na mBan. Among those armed and assembled on both sides of the main road were members of the Listry IRA, including Captain Daniel Allman, and the Callinafercy Company under Captain John ('Jack Captain') Heffernan, all of whom were comrades of Mulvihill and the men of the Milltown IRA. When Caseley and Evans appeared on their bicycles, Allman stepped onto the road and ordered them, at gunpoint, to halt. When the pair attempted to cycle onwards, they were fired upon. When the shooting stopped, Caseley had been killed outright but Evans lay injured on the road. According to eyewitness accounts, Allman then dragged Evans to where his dead comrade lay and ordered Ned Langford to shoot the dying man. When Langford refused to do so, Allman threatened to kill him and Langford's company captain, John Heffernan, was forced to intervene. Allman called on others present to 'finish off the Tan' and Evans was duly killed.[15]

Unsurprisingly, retaliation was swift. After police in Killorglin retrieved the bodies in the early hours of the following morning, 1 November, they proceeded to 'shoot up the town'. The Sinn Féin Hall at Lower Bridge Street, a garage, timber mill, the creamery and other buildings were burned. Shops and houses were raided and ransacked, and many families were forced to flee. Killorglin was described by local resident

Major Leeson-Marshall of Callinafercy as being 'like a city of the dead'.[16]

Mulvihill was in Tralee when the Hillville killings occurred. No doubt aware that the Crown forces would turn their attention to Milltown in reprisal for the deaths, he returned home and prepared to defend his community against retaliation. Just hours after Hillville, a group of Black and Tans arrived in the village. Shots were fired indiscriminately on the streets, forcing many women and children to flee to Kilcolman Abbey, home of Sir William Godfrey. Others barricaded themselves in the post office. Some took refuge in the Catholic Church – when the Black and Tans entered, they were ordered to leave by Fr Patrick Buckley, who called them murderers and looters. Several homes and businesses were attacked and set on fire. The local IRA suspected that the Black and Tans would return to Milltown that night, but by this time, they were prepared:

> Tom O'Connor, Battalion O/C had an idea they [the Crown forces] would come out again that night to burn Milltown and he got seventeen fellows who were able to get shotguns. We got enough cartridges to load them by peeling some of them that had swollen with damp. We went to Kilderry where there was a good position,[17] about 10.30pm, and waited. It was [a] clear, frosty night. About 1.30am we heard the noise of the Crossley [Tender] coming,[18] and as it arrived in front of us, someone shouted 'Halt'. They opened fire; so did we. The Crossley

> swerved out across the road, and out again, away along the main road and turned into a branch road back to Killorglin. We got up and ran as we had no ammunition left. We wounded three of them, none seriously, but we were very happy going home, we had been under fire. I think I got a greater kick out of that than anything else in the Tan time.

The incidents at Hillville and Kilderry represented an escalation in the brutality of reprisals, for which the Black and Tans became renowned. But they also reinvigorated the local IRA and, over the coming months, attacks against the Crown forces continued with increased intensity and ferocity.

+++

By the end of 1920, Mulvihill had been promoted to the rank of battalion adjutant and was overseeing preparations for ambushes and attacks on the Crown forces. He estimated that the battalion at this time consisted of some 'six hundred men'.[19] A new flying column of IRA members from the 6th Battalion was formed:

> The Brigade [Flying] Column started that week [November 1920] and from that to the Truce four of us were permanent members, Tom [O']Connor, Batt. O/C, myself (Batt. Adjutant), J. [Jimmy] Cronin and J. [Jack] Flynn. The Battalion started at Inch, across the Bay to

> Mountain Stage, south to Bealach Óisín, southeast to Bealach Béama, along Carrantuohill to Ballymalis and on to Milltown.[20] 'Twas one hell of a big area for footwork. We did not stay in the Hut at any time as we had seven companies to organise, and they expected you to visit at least once a month.

'The Hut' to which Mulvihill referred was an isolated hideout at Fybough in the Sliabh Mish mountains on the Dingle Peninsula. It was developed by necessity rather than design. Following the Siege of Tralee, many of the IRA leaders in the town went on the run and needed a hideout where they could evade the authorities but from where they could also launch attacks on the Crown forces. Under the leadership of O/C Paddy Cahill, the Tralee IRA established their base at the Hut, which was described by one of its occupants as 'a large wooden structure built at the back of a massive rock in the mountainside. It was well camouflaged and safe from enemy surprise. It commanded a view of the Dingle Peninsula and Castlemaine Bay, while to the back it afforded a way of retreat, if necessary ...'[21] Cahill and the Tralee men were catered for by members of Cumann na mBan from nearby Keel and Castlemaine, and they would be joined by other high-profile volunteers such as Tadhg Brosnan of Castlegregory and Johnny Connor of Farmers' Bridge. Though Mulvihill does not appear to have stayed at the Hut at any point, he was in regular contact with the men there as they plotted and planned their next engagements with the forces of the Crown:

> The fellows who were in the Hut were nearly all from Tralee. The Hut was in our Battalion HQ. It would be hard to meet a better bunch. They were nearly all officers who had been active. They included the Battalion O/Cs, Company O/Cs, Brigade O/Cs and Brigade Quarter Master. There were no supermen there. We never had any.

The men of the Hut would soon join Mulvihill in some of the most consequential and bloody engagements of the war against the Crown.

CHAPTER 3

'The good houses'

AS 1920 DREW TO a close and as the War of Independence entered its third year, Dan Mulvihill and his IRA comrades had settled into a stubborn pattern of tit-for-tat engagements with the enemy, with neither the republicans nor the Crown forces gaining the upper hand. The IRA, with the invaluable assistance of Cumann na mBan, continued to keep the Black and Tans and the Auxiliaries on the back foot. This was despite a limited supply of weapons and ammunition, which were often of a poor standard. Damp ammunition was a hazard, as was the manufacture and storage of buckshot and bullets. Mulvihill noted that 'the [IRA] Companies had nothing but old shotguns and bad cartridges and they failed to do any damage – at thirty feet'. This made it necessary to engage at closer range with a target when a shot was fired.

What the IRA might have lacked in good-quality armaments or ammunition, it made up for in other ways. One of the IRA's most essential weapons was often as deadly as any gun, grenade or bullet. The collection and use of detailed intelligence was absolutely integral to the war between 1919 and 1921. Monitoring the activities of police and soldiers, anticipating their movements, intercepting their communications, eavesdropping on their conversations in social settings and fraternising with off-duty officers and the rank and file proved crucially effective in tactical terms for the IRA.

One key source of intelligence for Dan Mulvihill and the 6th Battalion were the boys and young men of Fianna Éireann (the Irish National Boy Scouts). The brainchild of IRB leader Bulmer Hobson and Countess Markievicz, the Fianna was set up in 1909 as the youth wing of the revolutionary movement. The members would be directed by the IRA to monitor individuals or groups of soldiers or police and to report details to the local company. In Kerry, the organisation developed branches across the county, including a branch – or *sluagh* – which was aligned to Mulvihill's Milltown Company of the IRA.[1] Billy Keane from Castlemaine was 'Chief Scout' and fed information to Mulvihill on enemy movements. The intelligence of the Fianna would be vital to Mulvihill's prosecution of the war against the enemy.

Likewise, the way in which the members of Cumann na mBan were deployed to collect information and intelligence, by watching the movements of the Crown forces, spying or eavesdropping on soldiers and police in their own workplaces and relaying information to the IRA, was essential and extremely productive. Joan O'Brien (later O'Sullivan) was one of the most significant Cumann na mBan operatives in Kerry at the time and was someone whom Mulvihill came to rely on for intelligence gathering and communications. Mulvihill later hailed her as an 'active member' who was 'doing I.O. [intelligence officer] work' for the 6th Battalion.[2] O'Brien's home at Glencuttane in Glencar, about ten miles from Killorglin, was used as a divisional headquarters and a frequent meeting place for the IRA. O'Brien also acted as an unofficial postmaster, overseeing the receipt and relaying of important messages to IRA companies across the battalion: 'a message sent there [the O'Brien home] would always be sure to reach the officer for whom it was intended'.[3] O'Brien occupied a hugely valuable position in the community from an intelligence-gathering perspective – she was a barmaid in O'Shea's pub in Killorglin, which was frequented by policemen. It was claimed the O'Sheas were 'friendly with the enemy forces' and O'Brien used her position to observe 'the movements of the Black and Tan forces in the town, ascertaining their habits, the places they used to visit, etc., and reporting anything which she could learn to the IRA'.[4] Though O'Brien proved very effective in relaying information to Mulvihill and his men, her actions and those of other members of Cumann na mBan were not without significant consequences. She would suffer heavily for her activities when the Black and Tans set her home on fire in the hours after the Hillville ambush in October 1920. Remarkably, the incident further incentivised O'Brien to continue her republican activities, which she resumed on moving to Cahersiveen, where she worked diligently for the Kerry No. 3 Brigade.

Not only did the IRA and the women of Cumann na mBan observe, detect and eavesdrop on the Black and Tans and their counterparts, they also kept a close eye on civilians suspected of being sympathetic to the forces of the Crown or, even worse, providing them with information about the activities of the rebels. The informer occupies a much reviled and deeply detested space in Irish history. From 'Bird', the suspected informer in John B. Keane's *The Field*, to the very real 'Stakeknife', aka Freddie Scappaticci, during the Troubles in Northern Ireland, the history of Ireland is replete with examples of those who, for whatever reason, decided to tip off or talk to the other side. Being accused of or being found to be an informer or a spy could have lethal consequences and many of those suspected of spying for the enemy were attacked or killed.

Throughout the war, Mulvihill and the leaders of the Kerry brigades were suspicious of local civilians whom it was believed may be sympathetic to the Crown forces, or those believed to be supplying them with information about the rebels, their movements, hiding places and activities. Suspicions about those who were British nationals, agents or supporters of the Crown, or those – for nakedly sectarian reasons – who were members of the Church of Ireland, were relayed not only to local IRA commanders but also to general headquarters. The type of intelligence which Mulvihill and those under his command collected at this time is revealed in one of the lesser-known collections of documents held in the Military Archives at the Cathal Brugha Barracks in Dublin.

The so-called Collins Papers – named after IRA commander and Dáil minister General Michael Collins – contains a series of dispatches between IRA brigades and battalion officers and IRA headquarters, including senior figures such as Collins, Richard Mulcahy, Gearóid O'Sullivan and Cathal Brugha. Among the 228 files in the collection are reports from members of Mulvihill's 6th Battalion about those suspected of informing, including reports submitted on civilians in Mulvihill's company area in Milltown. They reveal the type of subterfuge, suspicion and sometimes paranoia that became typical of the war. Short reports on civilians who were suspected of acting as informants for the enemy were submitted to Dublin: 'John Hixon, Milltown: Out hunting, saw [IRA] Volunteers mobilising for ambush. Went to Tralee that night and informed Auxiliaries. Place was raided next day. Was to have been taken away if hostilities were resumed. Const Bergen [Bergin] gave above information before he left country. Was going with sister of above mentioned.'[5]

Cavorting with the enemy in a social setting was also deeply frowned upon and attracted the ire of the IRA:

> John Heffernan, Farmer, Callinafercy West, Milltown: Drinking with Tans. Got this [these] Tans to take Volunteer into Barracks and beat him badly. Volunteer who was beaten will prove charge.
>
> Michael Kelliher, Farmer, 47 years of age, stout, well built, fair moustache, ruddy complexion, good features, Callinafercy West, Milltown: Constantly drinking with R.I.C. Often seen in secret conversation with them, was heard to ask a policeman to burn the [word illegible] and farmyard of a volunteer who was on the run.[6]

A more pronounced degree of revulsion was reserved for women who developed relationships with members of the Crown forces and who were discovered not only to be romantically involved with the enemy but also suspected of sharing information with them:

> Mary Sullivan, Farmer's daughter, working on farm. Very tall, ruddy complexion, 24 years of age, dark hair. Callinafercy West, Milltown. Always keeping company with B and Tans. Gave them information about volunteers on the run – houses they were staying in etc. D O'Dwyer Killorglin and Constable Bergen [Bergin] will prove charges.[7]

The fate of women found by the IRA to be fraternising with police or soldiers was often the very same punishment meted out by the Crown forces to republican women. The cropping of hair – a visible sign that a woman had been adjudged an informer or was cavorting with the enemy – was a ritualistic punishment, which sometimes progressed to sexual assault.[8] There is no evidence to connect Dan Mulvihill with any such assaults on women in his own community, but he cannot have been oblivious to how traitors and informers, particularly women, were treated by many in his own ranks.

+++

Mulvihill's memoir provides insights into another integral ingredient in the IRA's ability to outsmart their opponents and to escape the clutches of the authorities on a regular basis: the use of a network of places to stay and hide while on the run. Few combatants remained in their own homes for too long, ever alert to the probability of a raid. Instead, if they were not using a dugout or a hideout like the Hut, they spent a few days and nights at a time at the home of an individual or family sympathetic to republicans. There, they could be assured of a hot meal, a change of clothes, a night's sleep and a chance to tend to any injuries or ailments before moving on to the next engagement. Many of what became known as 'safe houses' – or as Mulvihill called them, the 'good houses' – were located in remote and rural areas. This usually put those on the run beyond the reach or detection of the Black and Tans or the Auxiliaries, forces which, because they were made up of men unfamiliar with the landscape and were increasingly vulnerable to attack outside their urban barracks, rarely ventured into isolated areas or impenetrable terrain.

If the volunteers and members of Cumann na mBan needed an ideal location to evade detection and arrest, then they found it in the parish of Glencar, a sprawling, sparsely populated and mountainous area at the foot of Ireland's highest mountain, Carrauntoohil. The remoteness and relative isolation of the area provided IRA volunteers with a network of hideouts and places to meet, train and recuperate. Glencar was home to a number of Mulvihill's 'good houses':

> Now, I am going to tell you about something else: the good houses. There were a couple of dozen in Glencar,

and about half a dozen in each of the other Companies. My first visit to Glencar was in November, 1920 ... I had seen a lot of beautiful places in the world, mostly tropical, but I had never seen anything to touch Glencar as it was at the time. From the top of the parish to the hotel at [the] foot of Caragh Lake was one riot of colour. It was the most beautiful place I had ever seen. All the trees were deciduous, and the tints of autumn made a fairyland of it all.

The people of Glencar were out on their own. They loved to have fellows on the run amongst them, and they went out of their way to find things to do for them. There had been a police barracks there until early June 1920. The local company ambushed a patrol, wounded two of them and got two rifles, a long Lee Enfield and a Police Carbine. The police pulled out the week after and Glencar became a small Republic.[9]

The battalion area took in some very famous places. Caherconree, where the fortress still remains, as it must have been long before Cú Rí Mac Daire was heard of.[10] We can place him. He ruled in Kerry about the time of the Crucifixion as it was some time previous to that he had his scrap with Cú Chullain.[11] On the other end we had Carrantuohill, at its foot Derrynafeena, and two famous passes, Bealach Béama and Bealach Óisín.[12]

If one Kerry homestead became synonymous with the fight for Irish independence at this time it was the home of the Daly family at Knockaneacoolteen, a small townland about halfway between Castlemaine and Firies, which Mulvihill hailed as one of the most important homesteads of the revolutionary years. Members of the family became household names in Ireland, principal among them Charlie Daly – or Dálaigh, as the family were better known. His brothers were IRA volunteers and their sister, May (Mai), was an active member of Cumann na mBan. She was a Sinn Féin candidate in Kerry South at the 1957 general election. For Mulvihill, the Daly's ranked highly among his heroes:

> Outstanding from 1916 to the present time, it [the Dálaigh home] was a focal point for all of Ireland and never a very safe place to visit. It had been the centre of the I.R.A. in Kerry for over sixty years and was raided by all political parties for fifty-eight of the sixty. The two missing years are the year of the Truce [1921–22] and the year that Fianna Fáil got into power [1932]. The house [was] burned in May 1921. Jack Shanahan was shot there that day (he recovered years later).[13] From 1922 to 1932, the raids were weekly and sometimes daily. A good lot of fellows were beaten up there. A Clare man, Sean Ryan got out worst. I think George Gilmore was caught there also.[14] I am not sure of Sean Mac Bride, he was Tom's pal.[15] Charlie was O/C of the 2nd Northern Division pre-Truce. The Free State executed him at Drumboe on 14th March 1923 ... The eldest brother Bill [Willie] Daly died in '43 or '44. Cornelius, the youngest died in the fifties. They

> all died as they lived: I.R.A. Their house was raided by the Tans, Auxiliaries, R.I.C. Free State, Fianna Fáil, Coalition, Fianna Fáil, Coalition, Fianna Fáil, Coalition – not a bad record for sixty years. Who wouldn't be a patriot? Well, they are all gone, with the passing of May Daly [1982], the last.

During 1920, the Mulvihill home itself became a 'good house', like many of those in Glencar and elsewhere, and it became a focal point for the local IRA and the members of Cumann na mBan in the mid-Kerry area. Because Castlemaine straddled the boundary between the Kerry No. 1 and No. 2 Brigades, Mulvihills' offered a suitable meeting point for the commanders and members of those brigades. It also provided respite for the men and a useful focal point for communications, all of which Dan's sister, Katie, was heavily involved in. She described her activities during 1920 in the following way:

> Cooked for and kept in house members of I.R.A. Kept arms and ammunition for members of the Brigade Column. Nursed J. [Jimmy] Cronin, Kerry 1 Column when injured in winter of 1920 ... Carried dispatches and received and arranged for delivery of dispatches. House was centre for receiving dispatches from Kerry 2 for Kerry 1 Brigade H.Q. and Kerry 1 Column.[16]

The names of those who stayed in the Mulvihill home at this time provide evidence of its importance as a safe house and also point to the integral role that Dan and Katie – along with their mother, Nora, and sister, Bridie – played in the War of Independence at this time. Katie's testimony, provided many decades later to the Pensions Board of the Department of Defence, included the names of those who found refuge at Brackhill and who stayed in Katie's care while they were trying to evade the forces of the Crown:

- Dan and Pat Allman, members of the Listry (4th Battalion) IRA, from Rockfield to the east of Milltown, came from a staunchly republican family which became immersed in the Volunteers from the outset. Their sister May was O/C of the Milltown Company of Cumann na mBan and their brother, Fr Myles, was an outspoken member of the clergy who later became active in Fianna Fáil.[17] Dan Allman is most remembered as one of those killed at the Headford Junction ambush in March 1921. Pat Allman, who became O/C of the 4th Battalion, would later play an active role in the anti-Treaty IRA during the Civil War.

- Jack Shanahan was a member of a well-known republican family from Castleisland. His brother, Richard (Dick), was a key member of his local battalion and was killed during an IRA attack on an army patrol on 11 July 1921, the final day of the War of Independence. Jack, a chemist, was wounded during a raid on the Dálaigh home in Firies in May 1921.

- Gregory Ashe, from Kinard, Lispole, joined the Volunteers after he returned from a period in the United States and became a key member of Kerry No. 1 Brigade. His brother, Thomas Ashe, led the Volunteers in the north Dublin area during the Easter Rising and was their leader at the so-called Battle of Ashbourne in County Meath in the days which followed. Thomas died shortly after being force-fed in Mountjoy Prison on 25 September 1917, while he was on hunger strike, and became a republican martyr.

Like these details from Katie, if her brother's memoir is noteworthy for anything, it is for providing an extensive list of names of those involved in the armed struggle in this period, particularly those in his own battalion. Until the publication of the rolls of members of various units of the IRA and Cumann na mBan by the Military Archives in recent years, accurate details of the actual membership of these bodies were often sporadic and imprecise. The witness statements gathered by the Bureau of Military History in the 1940s and 1950s – which were locked away by the Department of the Taoiseach until 2001 – do provide names of many of the protagonists; however, for many years, the true extent of the republican rank and file at this time remained underestimated and lacking many of the details of membership. Moreover, there was often lingering doubt among families and communities about whether a relative or a neighbour was involved in the revolution, due to the prevailing silence preserved by many combatants, who chose, for a variety of reasons, to say little, if anything, about a traumatic and turbulent period in Irish history.

Mulvihill's memoir offers details of the IRA companies which made up the 6th Battalion for much of the War of Independence and supplements archive records and other accounts from the time:

> I am going to write about my own Battalion, the Sixth Battalion, Kerry No. 2 [Brigade]. It was a Battalion of Kerry 1 up to 21st June, 1921. I think every fellow thinks his own was the best. We had seven companies. Eight Company O/Cs. That is to include Joe Taylor who was murdered in February 1921.[18] The eight were – Joe Taylor, followed by his brother Jim, Glencar;[19] Frank Grady, Glenbeigh;[20] Mick Dwyer, Caragh Lake; Jimmy Foley, Killorglin; Mick Scully, Dungeel; John Heffernan, Milltown; and Tim Sullivan, Kilgobnet.
>
> Joe Taylor was murdered by Tans. Jim Taylor and Frank Grady were murdered by Free State troops. Mick Dwyer was killed in [a] fight in Fossa during the Civil War.[21] Jimmie Foley and Mick Scully died of T.B. Tim Sullivan died last year (1976) in Australia. John Heffernan died Spring, 1977. Tom [O']Connor, Batt O/C, was a member of the Column [the] whole time. He was in the Column in the Civil War, wounded in Kilmallock, end of July, 1922.[22]
>
> Bertie Scully was Vice O/C: his brother Liam was killed in an attack on Kilmallock 1920.[23] Other brother

> was in Ballykinlar [internment camp in County Down]. Bertie was attached to Division Staff and was wounded in Civil War. He died as he lived: I.R.A. Paddy 'Rua' Sullivan Q.M. [Quartermaster] had been in the goldfields in Australia, came home on holidays and was into the fight straight away. Paddy was an adjutant. Outside of the fellows I have mentioned, there were a number of other officers with us on the run. Batty Dwyer, who became Company O/C Killorglin after J. Foley; Martin Wade, Brigade Engineer; Tom Sullivan Batt. Engineer; Bill Wade.[24] There were a whole lot of others in the Companies.

The names of many of those 'others' would be provided by Mulvihill when he wrote and typed copious lists of names and addresses of company members for the Department of Defence, particularly for a collection known as the Brigade Activity Reports, which lists those involved in the various ambushes and incidents of the time. The reports were a key source of information for officials who would adjudicate on the pension applications of combatants and their relatives between the 1930s and 1950s. Importantly, Mulvihill also provides some names of the members of Cumann na mBan, although not to the same extent as those of the IRA:

> Now to the Cumann na mBan. Maureen O'Shea, Killorglin (her aunt was married to Doctor Ryan) was a grand singer. One of the original Kerry Feis Troupe that carried

> on during 1917, 1918, 1919. She was a courier to London and sang at all the St. Patrick's Night Concerts there up to 1930.[25] Joan O'Brien, Glencar was on the run during the time of the Tans from November, 1920 and again in Civil War. Two Wades from Killorglin.[26] Two Breens, Kilgobnet. Dr. Marie Foley, Killorglin, who died on the run in 1923. I met one of the Breens thirty-two years later, she was Reverend Mother of the Bon Secours Hospital in Glasnevin. They are all dead now.

Though the names of members of Cumann na mBan are few in Mulvihill's memoir, they were manifold in the records and letters that he was required to provide when those women applied for a range of pensions and allowances in recognition of their work as volunteers.

+++

The Crown forces had their spies and their informers too, and the house at Brackhill inevitably came to the attention of the authorities. The Black and Tans and the Auxiliaries visited the locality with increased regularity following their rampage through Milltown on 1 November 1920 in retaliation for the events at Hillville. Local homes became a target for raids, indiscriminate shooting and arson. The home of Katie Mulvihill's comrade in Cumann na mBan, Maggie Slattery, who lived near Milltown, was set ablaze and she was taken to jail at Ballymullen Barracks in Tralee. She was hauled before the Auxiliary leader in Kerry, Major Mackinnon, who ripped a rosary from around her neck. She was verbally and physically abused and may have met a worse fate but for the intervention of the local curate, Fr Sandy O'Sullivan.[27]

Shortly before Christmas 1920, a group of Auxiliaries raided the Mulvihill home, but it was spared being set ablaze like so many others. The only account of the raid is provided in the testimony of Katie Mulvihill, and she does not detail who was home or what occurred. There were no known arrests, but crucially, Katie managed to leave before the raiders arrived. Likely acting on a tip-off or showing the guile for which she was renowned, she 'managed to get away with [a] haversack containing revolvers and ammunition'.[28] The failure to discover any weapons or bullets, which Dan and Katie regularly stashed in the hayshed and the rafters, may have saved the house, and the Auxiliaries may have hoped that the raid would deter the Mulvihills from their paramilitary activities. If anything, it had the opposite effect and propelled Dan Mulvihill into even more violent and dangerous engagements with the enemy.

CHAPTER 4

'Until he bled to death'

AT THE BEGINNING OF 1921, Ireland was facing into a third year of war between Irish republicans and the forces of the British Crown. In Kerry, despite the bolstering of the RIC with the deployment of the Auxiliaries and the Black and Tans, the Crown forces showed no meaningful sign of getting a grip on the IRA and bringing the conflict to an end. This was also despite a new 'shoot to kill' policy, which was introduced by British Army officers and senior police figures and which came to typify the lawless brutality of the Black and Tans, in particular in the later months of 1920 and into 1921. In a notorious address to his men at various barracks in Kerry during 1920, the Divisional Commissioner for Munster, Gerald Bryce Ferguson Smyth, had declared, 'The more you shoot, the better I will like you, and I assure you that no policeman will get into trouble for shooting any man.'[1] Another of those lectures had been delivered at Milltown RIC Barracks and, in a sign of growing tensions and divisions within the ranks, prompted one constable to abuse the commissioner and storm out.[2]

In February 1921 Dan Mulvihill was appointed intelligence officer of the Kerry No. 2 Brigade and was responsible, as the name suggests, for the gathering and dissemination of information about the movements of the Crown forces.[3] Energised and enthused by the ongoing stalemate and by the success of several ambushes and attacks, the IRA in mid-Kerry became more ambitious and daring. Having forced the police to abandon rural outposts like Milltown, Glencar and Boolteens, the focus turned to the larger urban garrisons to which the RIC and their counterparts had withdrawn for defensive reasons. The district headquarters at Killorglin were the target for repeated attacks by Mulvihill and his men in the early months of 1921:

> We started, after Christmas [1920], making arrangements for [an] attack on a [police] patrol that left Killorglin about five nights a week, and came over the Laune Bridge. The area facing the bridge where the new cottages now are was an open field with a round ditch running out the Killarney road.[4] I think it was [the] first or second week of February before the final arrangements were made. We brought eight fellows from Glencar, about a dozen from local Companies and [the] Column crossed the ferry at Callinafercy.[5]
>
> We took up positions facing the bridge and waited. Nothing turned up. Jimmy Cronin and myself went into town and found that they [the RIC/Black and Tans] had

> left town about seven [o'clock] in plain clothes, went out Glenbeigh road. We went back and [the] crowd packed up. I asked two Glencar fellows to come with me and have a sleep until they could go home in the morning. They were Joe Taylor and Paddy Murphy. Joe said, 'No, Dan, we will go home first and sleep after.' We all went our different ways. I never saw Joe again. He was buried before we heard of what had happened. Joe and Paddy arrived in Glencar. Paddy shot off for Lickeen and home. Joe went home and threw his haversack on the table, went to take off his shoes and fell asleep. Just at dawn the Tans burst in the door, took him down to the White Gate, made him climb on [the] fence and shot him. They kept the local women back until he bled to death.

The killing of IRA volunteer Joe Taylor in Glencar in February 1921 was one of the most vicious and controversial of the war in Kerry. According to contemporaneous accounts, on his return to his home at Lyranes in rural Glencar, Taylor fell asleep. The police patrol that had earlier left Killorglin was bound for the area, unknown to Taylor and his comrades. Dressed in civilian clothing, the Crown forces entered the Taylor home and took Joe into custody. Taylor was shot in the thigh and haemorrhaging badly when, according to Bertie Scully of the Glencar IRA, one officer attempted first aid but soon fled the scene. Taylor did receive medical treatment from a local doctor, but it was to no avail: he was dead within an hour. Among the patrol of RIC and Black and Tans was Constable

Joseph Cooney, who, it was claimed, dragged Taylor from his home.[6] It was shortly after this incident that the RIC decided their barracks in Glencar was no longer safe and, amid the rising tensions, it was abandoned. Cooney and his colleagues, it was alleged, were extremely bitter at being forced to leave the area.[7] Their involvement in Joe Taylor's death would have deadly consequences for them, and the incident at Lyranes in the early hours of 27 February 1921 would reverberate all the way to a major ambush a few short months later.

+++

Infuriated by Taylor's death, within days Mulvihill and other IRA members made a daring retaliatory assassination attempt in Killorglin. Along with Mulvihill, Jimmy Cronin, Jack Flynn, Tom O'Connor and Denis Quirke entered the home of the local RIC head constable, Blake. He had already been fired upon by the IRA when they 'searched all the pubs for Tans' in Killorglin during an assault on the town in January 1921. This time, a more direct approach was adopted. A detailed account of the incident was provided by Jimmy Cronin of the Milltown IRA:

> The Sergeant whom we intended to kidnap did not live in the barracks. He was married and lived in a private house by the side of the river near the bridge but our information regarding the location of his house was poor. There were three houses standing together and we knew he lived in one of them. We prepared the job by placing two scouts

> on the bridge and three of us were to go to the houses, one to each door to knock at the same time to avoid alarming the Sergeant. I took the first house, Dan Mulvihill the second and Denis Quirke the third. I lifted the latch of the first house, the door being unlocked, and a woman came to the door. I knew I was at the wrong house. Just as I was moving from the door I heard Dan Mulvihill give a shout. He had lifted the latch on the second house and seen the Sergeant's cap hanging on the stairs. We all rushed for the second house. The Sergeant was upstairs with his wife who had had a baby. A little boy came down on to the stairs as we entered. We called on the Sergeant to come down but Jack Flynn (T.D.) fired a shot (I don't know for what reason) and Thomas O'Connor gave us the order to get out. The shot had given the alarm and we had to cross the bridge to get out of the town.[8]

According to Mulvihill, the repercussions of the killing of Joe Taylor did not end there:

> Early in March [1921], we made preparations for a big attack on Killorglin. This was a Brigade Column operation. We had about sixty men, and took up positions all over the town. I was with Brigade O/C in the Ball Alley facing Iveragh Road. A patrol coming [was] attacked and we had a scrap for about half an hour in the dark. I think they just faded out and got to the barracks by laneways. We attacked the barracks but it was useless.

During this incident, the IRA set themselves up in the front rooms of some of the houses near the barracks with the occupants, according to one newspaper report, being 'politely but firmly' ordered into their back rooms.[9] From the houses, the attackers began to shoot at a patrol. 'We knew that we couldn't take the barracks,' said Tom O'Connor, the officer in command, 'but the idea was to give mostly the men experience!'[10] The incident represented an increasing confidence among the IRA rank and file who, according to a report in the *Kerry People*, 'marched from the town at an early hour, having suffered no casualties'.[11]

Shortly afterwards, Mulvihill and the Milltown IRA began to work more closely with their comrades at the Hut, all of whom were experienced and battle-hardened volunteers, ever eager for the fight since their banishment from Tralee in November 1920. The men there were led by Paddy Cahill, with whom Mulvihill engaged more and more as the war progressed. Cahill was O/C Kerry No. 1 Brigade and was one of the most senior IRA leaders in the county. His background and experience in the republican movement in Kerry was extensive. His cinema in Tralee was destroyed by the Black and Tans during one of their many sacks of the town. Now nursing his wounds with his comrades on the west Kerry mountainside, he was keen to take the fight once more to the enemy. With Mulvihill, he plotted a series of deadly ambushes in the spring of 1921.

+++

The Lispole ambush was one of the better-known incidents of the War of Independence in Kerry, and Mulvihill was central to its preparations as well as its execution.[12] Along with Jack Flynn, Jimmy Cronin and Thomas O'Connor, he was invited to meet Paddy Cahill in March 1921, at which meeting Cahill told them 'of his plan to attack a Black & Tan patrol on the Dingle to Tralee road at Lispole'.[13] Mulvihill described what followed on 22 March 1921:

> ... the Brigade Column decided to have a go at a patrol that left Dingle, either Tuesday or Wednesday and came on to Lispole and Annascaul. Tom [O']Connor and myself went to Glencar for rifles. The four of us joined about twenty-five miles and it was just dusk as we got to Annascaul. I remember we got absolution from a priest at the railway station, and we then went on to Lispole. Tom O'Connor and myself were billeted at Ashes, Kinard.[14] A brother of Tom Ashe: his son was in the fight with us. There was a disused school overlooking the road and about twenty feet back. I had seventeen men there: they were all armed with shotguns loaded with heavy buckshot, and were to open the attack. The main Column were along the hillside to the back of the school.
>
> We waited in position for two days. The second day, most of us wanted to move into position nearer town. After long debate it was decided to wait until the next day and to move in the evening if nothing showed up. They turned up alright, but not as we wanted them to.

Some woman who went into town mentioned having seen fellows on the road at Lispole. They landed help that evening by sea and the following day came out within a mile, came around at [the] back of hill, along the fold to the north and surrounded us. I know we had scouts out, but I don't know, to this day, what happened.

Our first indication of trouble was machine gun bullets tearing through the slate of the school roof. I could see them advancing in [the] valley about a mile away. The school was their objective, and they took their time about it. One crowd would open up with [the] machine gun and another crowd would advance to a new position. We sat and took it as it was no good opening up with shotguns and telling them we were there. They kept on coming and a rifle grenade hit the gable. They were right into the position of the Column and they opened up on them. About six of them were wounded and three of our fellows. The Tans retreated to a lorry which had advanced to [a] height on the road west of [the] village. There was a dead calm.

I got to the window and could see the lorry turning on the road and decided they were coming to get us and we got the whole lot to the windows to give them everything we had. After about five minutes the Crossley [Tender] had made no move and I told the boys to hold their positions and I would go out and try to find out what way we stood. I had only gone about ten yards when I found a Tan who had been shot through the legs. I saw that he was alright and went on, and met a scout who told me that the O/C sent him to tell me to get the fellows out, as they were retreating. I went back to the school and got the fellows out and found that we would have to cross open space west of the chapel and jump a small stream under full view of the church wall. I thought they could not all escape. They were all across and I was not too happy taking the run and jump by myself.

It was getting dark and when we joined the main group we found some missing. We went back again and found other fellows bringing out two badly wounded. We retreated towards Annascaul and got cars to take the two wounded. Tommie Hawley had a head wound and was unconscious.[15] Tom Ashe, in whose house we had stayed, had a wound in the groin and was smoking and talking and he suddenly slumped over dead.[16] He had bled to death internally. Tommie Hawley lingered on but eventually died. Jimmie Daly, Castlegregory, wounded through the shoulder and chest, walked along with me until we came to a safe house.[17] (I met him last September as he was returning to the States, our first meeting in fifty years.) We stayed in a local house that night and started for home the following evening. Four of us walked the twenty-five miles home. I went to bed and was asleep when a boy came with the account that I had been killed at Lispole. He had heard it at the creamery.

Early the following morning, as they arrived at Rae's Hotel in Boolteens near Castlemaine – a well-known meeting point for the local IRA – Mulvihill and his comrades heard of the death the previous day of Dan Allman in an ambush at Headford Junction in east Kerry, the most high-profile incident in the war in Kerry. They travelled to Aglish cemetery near Listry for the interment and one of the largest funerals that Kerry had ever seen. Allman became an icon, the image on his mortuary card remaining one of the most instantly recognisable of the War of Independence.

A month later, in April 1921, Paddy Cahill provided instructions for the next engagement with the enemy, inviting Mulvihill and Tom O'Connor, along with Billy Mullins from Tralee, to a meeting near Camp on the northern side of the Dingle Peninsula:

> We stayed in the area for the night. The following day as we came up the Maum,[18] we turned to the right for Caherconree and when we got to what I call Fionn Mac Cumhaill's Table,[19] we sat on the mountain overlooking the valley. Paddy Cahill pointed across the bay [Castlemaine Harbour] to Glenbeigh and said that would be our next objective. We decided that it would be a hush-hush operation, as information was leaking out all the time. We sent a young lad (Fianna) from Tralee, whose father was from the area. It took nearly a month to make all the arrangements. We came from Glencar by boat through Caragh Lake and went by foreshore, from Dooks to

> Glenbeigh. The [Flying] Column crossed the bay and we all met before dawn. We went into the [railway] station and took up every available position.

The attack at Glenbeigh on 26 April 1921 was designed to secure weapons and ammunition as well as a machine gun, which was known to be in the possession of the local constabulary. Mulvihill's statement to the Bureau of Military History decades later summarised what followed:

> Two men had previously gone on to Mountain Stage [the next station] to delay the train for ten minutes so that we would probably get the soldiers before the train arrived. Nine soldiers armed with rifles, one machine gunner with a Lewis Gun, and a soldier with spare pans of stuff for [the] gun, landed into the Station as the train was due. The whole crowd jumped out on them. They dumped all their stuff on the ground and ran for the Barracks. A couple of shots were fired over them to make them hurry up. No shots were fired from the Barracks, which was a couple of hundred yards away. One Lewis Gun, nine rifles and nearly two thousand rounds of .303 were captured. We retreated back the way we came, the main body crossing the Bay to Keel.[20]

The ambush – and haul of weapons – at Glenbeigh was one of Mulvihill's proudest moments of the war and fifty years later, in 1971, he published an account of the incident in *The*

Kerryman newspaper. He described the ambush as 'one of the most successful operations of Kerry No. 1 Brigade during the fight for freedom'.[21]

+++

The ambushes at Lispole and Glenbeigh coincided with significant structural and organisational changes in the IRA in Kerry. These reforms were instigated by a man with whom Mulvihill would have an increasingly close relationship, the O/C of the 1st Southern Division of the IRA, General Liam Lynch.[22] Lynch was one of the foremost figures in the Irish revolution and had risen rapidly through the ranks of the IRA. A native of Anglesborough, County Limerick, he joined the volunteers in Fermoy, County Cork, became commandant of the Cork No. 2 Brigade and led many successful attacks on the Crown forces. By the beginning of 1921, such was his reputation as a tactician and a leader of men that he was promoted to the divisional role, which put him in charge of nine brigades across Munster, including those in Kerry. In late April 1921 he travelled to Kerry to propose a restructuring of the three brigades and, controversially, to initiate some changes in personnel.

According to his biographer, Gerard Shannon, Lynch was 'particularly aggrieved' at the commander of the Kerry No. 1 Brigade, Paddy Cahill, who now operated from the Hut on the Dingle Peninsula.[23] Cahill's level of activity – or inactivity – at this point in the War of Independence, remains controversial. IRA headquarters was in receipt of reports of a sense of disorganisation and lethargy in the Kerry IRA and especially in Cahill's No. 1 Brigade. Reports from a GHQ officer suggested that Kerry battalions were working independently of each other and that there was little proper training, and claimed that only 10 per cent of volunteers could use a rifle. Referring to Cahill's flying column, the report noted that it seemed to be devoting its energies to 'eating, sleeping and general amusements'.[24] But despite these frustrations, Cahill continued to instigate and be involved in attacks on the forces of the Crown and he retained a loyal following, particularly within the Tralee IRA volunteers who were based at the Hut.

Lynch had another motivation too: the IRA was intent on removing the influence of the IRB in the higher ranks of the organisation. Cahill had been a senior member of the IRB in Tralee since before the Easter Rising.[25]

It was at Camp, a small village west of Tralee, that Lynch arrived in April 1921 to discuss the changes with senior officers in Kerry.[26] He was joined there by Éamon (Bob) Price, Director of Organisation from GHQ.[27] Dan Mulvihill travelled to the meeting 'with Paddy Cahill, Billy Mullins and Tom [O']Connor'. Though Mulvihill does not detail his version of events, an account of the meeting was provided by Bertie Scully, a senior figure in the Glencar IRA:

> In Camp, across the mountains Liam Lynch came down ... we got a boat to Keel and there we went across the mountains to Camp. There was a terrible crowd there, all the Bns [Battalions] ... Liam Lynch announced that

> Paddy Cahill was suspended. No one said a word and I had an empty feeling about it. 'If this means that one old O/C has been superseded,' I said, 'wouldn't it be good to have reasons for it?' Liam Lynch got red in the face and said: 'This is an order' and I sat down ...[28]

Scully's questioning of the orders of such a senior figure was indicative of widespread dissent in the ranks. Most of Cahill's men, including those at the Hut, refused allegiance to his replacement, Andy Cooney. A native of County Tipperary, Cooney was not a popular choice and was considered an outsider. As one of those members, Billy Mullins noted, 'all of us known as "Cahill's men" absolutely refused to serve under the new man'.[29]

As Lynch continued his tour of the Kerry brigades, he summoned senior officers in Kerry No. 2 and No. 3 Brigades to a meeting. The location chosen was the Mulvihill home at Brackhill. The venue for the meeting pointed not only to the geographical suitability of Mulvihills' as a safe place in which to hold such a significant gathering but also indicated how influential Mulvihill had become, as well as his increasingly close relationship with the head of the 1st Southern Division, the most influential IRA leader in Munster. Among those summoned to the meeting were Humphrey 'Free' Murphy, the head of the Kerry No. 2 Brigade, and Jeremiah (Jerome) Riordan, who was leader of the Kerry No. 3 Brigade. Murphy was an IRA lynchpin in his native east Kerry. The Currow native had been promoted to brigade O/C at the beginning of 1921 and thus took charge of a vast swathe of east and south Kerry, including Killarney, Kenmare, Castleisland and Killorglin. He would go on to vigorously oppose the Anglo-Irish Treaty of December 1921 and play a leading role in the Civil War. Also present was a man with whom Mulvihill would develop a lifelong friendship. Florence (Florrie) O'Donoghue of Rathmore on the Cork–Kerry border was a member of the Cork No. 1 Brigade and was an adjutant and intelligence officer with the 1st Southern Division. The working relationship and friendship between Mulvihill and O'Donoghue would long outlast the War of Independence.

Mulvihill remembered not only the significance of the meeting at Brackhill but also the somewhat comedic efforts to ensure that those attending had dry clothing:

> ... we were asked to make out a safe house for a Division meeting as Liam Lynch was coming to the area. Liam was the most wanted man in Ireland. It was decided to hold it at my house ... This was the best guarded meeting ever held in Kerry. There were scouts within sight of each other all the way to Tralee, Killarney, Killorglin and Farranfore. It was ... a very wet evening when I went to meet them. 'Free' Murphy was no bother as my clothes would fit him, we were the one height, 6'2". Florrie Donoghue was average and the suit of a boy we had working for us fitted him. Liam [Lynch] got the pants and coat of a brother of mine. I can still see him holding the pants under his armpits. My brother was 6'6" but the clothes were only needed while their own were drying.

Katie Mulvihill was responsible for looking after Lynch while he stayed at Brackhill and recorded who was present overnight: 'Liam Lynch, Div. O/C, F. [O']Donoghue, Div. Adjt., Free Murphy, O/C Kerry 2., and J. Riordan, O/C Kerry 3., stayed in house that night.'[30]

Dan Mulvihill clearly made a strong impression on Lynch: 'When Liam was leaving, he asked me if I would come on Division Staff later on. I said I would. I thought it was the greatest thing that ever happened – to be asked.' The invitation to take a more senior rank in the IRA would soon be accepted and would mark a significant escalation in Mulvihill's role in the fight against British rule.

CHAPTER 5

'Mad to get the chance'

FOR THE MEN AND women who joined the fight for Irish freedom in the early 1920s, the prospect of injury and death was always present. Dan Mulvihill and his family had provided shelter and comfort for the wounded and been to the funerals of fallen comrades all too often. Death was familiar. And if the possibility of injury and death was omnipresent, so too was the prospect of having to kill in the name of the republican cause. There is no available evidence that Mulvihill was directly responsible for the death of any member of the Crown forces before the summer of 1921. But all of that was about to change. By the beginning of the summer of 1921, the actual temperature, as well as the political temperature, was rising dramatically. May 1921 was characterised as a month of 'hot, cloudless days'[1] – the military situation was just as heated. 'It was,' recalled Ned Horan of the Firies IRA, a contemporary of Dan Mulvihill, 'very hot all during '21.'[2]

With positions hardening and both sides becoming more entrenched, the men and women of the volunteers in mid-

Kerry were about to engage in one of the war's most pivotal incidents and one which contributed to hastening the end of the war a few weeks later. Mulvihill and his accomplices had long been looking for an opportunity to carry out an ambush on a police patrol and were keen to capitalise on their successes at Glenbeigh and elsewhere. One such opportunity arose in the final days of May, as Mulvihill recalled:

> On the morning of the 25th May, Mick Galvin (Fianna) came running with an account of ten men from Killorglin Barracks passing through to Tralee. I sent him for Jimmy Cronin and Jack Flynn who were in [the] house nearby.[3] I sent J. Flynn through to Tim Brick, Company O/C, the two Barretts and Denny Quirke, 1st Lt. and told him that we would meet them at Castlemaine.[4] Jimmy Cronin went on to Keel where Tom [O']Connor was staying. I told him to tell Tom we would meet him on the Keel road.[5] Jimmy contacted Tom and a man was sent on to the Hut for arms and assistance. The Lewis Gun was at the Hut. I could use it and I was mad to get the chance. Flynn and the boys arrived at Castlemaine bridge and we went along the Keel road and met Tom and two others. They were waiting for word from the Hut. We were still waiting when Mick Galvin arrived to tell us that the Tans had returned home.

Mulvihill was livid that the IRA had missed an opportunity to ambush the police party: 'I cannot put into words how we felt. When we were parting I told Tom if they [the Tans] came again we would carry it out on our own.' His annoyance, which he was writing about almost sixty years after these events, stemmed from a frustration with the inaction and indecision of Paddy Cahill, who was still in charge, in name at least, of the men at the Hut in Fybough. Though he had been involved in the incidents in Lispole and Glenbeigh, Cahill appears to have become increasingly paralysed by indecision and, according to some accounts, poor health. Mulvihill and the senior figures in the 6th Battalion became dismayed by Cahill's reluctance to sanction attacks. They decided to take matters into their own hands and would no longer wait for Cahill's imprimatur if the opportunity to attack the Crown forces presented itself again.

Mulvihill was in receipt of ever-increasing and reliable intelligence from his spies in Fianna Éireann and Cumann na mBan about the movements and travel patterns of the RIC and their counterparts who were based at the divisional headquarters in Killorglin, the only police barracks remaining in mid-Kerry. It was intelligence he was keen to act on before those travel habits changed. The mode of travel was often a bicycle, which did not provide the cover or protection of a car or truck and made military and police movements vulnerable to attack. The bicycle was often chosen by necessity rather than design. The IRA had become increasingly successful at hindering the movement of military vehicles by cutting roads: this involved digging a deep trench across a road, often under cover of darkness, which was wide enough to prevent it from being traversed. Trees were also cut down to block roads. Forcing a vehicle to a halt in this way provided the perfect opportunity for an ambush or required the patrol to divert onto another road where an ambush had been laid. The extent of the cutting of roads in the mid-Kerry area in the early months of 1921 is evident in extracts from the diaries of Major Leeson-Marshall, who lived at Callinafercy House:

> *27 February – Sunday* – Road trenched again & trees felled across that Kilderry Wood. M [his wife, Meriel] did not go to church. I took [the] pony through Abbey road.
>
> *27 April – Wednesday* – Roads blocked at Milltown by felling trees & trench said to be 20ft wide cut across Killorglin to Killarney road at Ballymalis & one 12 ft. wide across Milltown to Killarney one.[6]

The Kerry County Inspector of the RIC had reported to headquarters in Dublin that the IRA had 'trenched all roads, blew up bridges, tore up railway lines, felled trees across roads, built up walls across roads, with the intention of making journeys of Crown Forces by motors impossible'.[7] Mulvihill and his comrades were keen to exploit this vulnerability.

+++

The men of the Killorglin garrison had been in the sights of the IRA for some time, among them the local district inspector, Michael Francis McCaughey, who, as a Black and Tan commander, was particularly loathed. One of the few Black and

Tans based there, Patrick Foley, was another 'much sought-after scalp'.[8] A native of Inch in west Kerry, Foley had been the first to the scene of the Hillville ambush and had spoken to *The Cork Examiner* about the incident: he was, Gregory Ashe noted, a 'bad peeler'.[9] Mulvihill knew that McCaughey and his men continued to cycle regularly to and from Tralee and, following the botched effort of 25 May 1921, he was determined not to miss a second opportunity. He also discovered that the police party had financial rather than military or policing motivations for their regular trips to Tralee: they needed to get to police headquarters to collect their pay. With others, he moved swiftly to prepare for another opportunity to attack:

> I told him [Mick Galvin, Fianna Éireann] I would have two hundred new cartridges loaded for the end of the week. We had made the powder, and I had got a mould and [a] good strip of lead. Three of us started on it the following day [26 May] in my house: Mossie Casey [and] Mick Scully, Company O/C, Dungeel ... We had only ten cartridges left without loading on Saturday night.

The IRA did not have to wait long. On 1 June 1921 the opportunity came and with it, one of the most dramatic and bloody encounters between the volunteers and the forces of the Crown in County Kerry.[10] At about nine o'clock, a party of twelve RIC and Black and Tans left Killorglin RIC Barracks for Tralee. Under the command of District Inspector McCaughey, they cycled in pairs through Milltown and Castlemaine, where they were easily spotted by IRA informants. Mulvihill was in the kitchen at Brackhill making buckshot when news of the police movement arrived:

> Mick Galvin arrived and said they [the Crown forces] had gone to town [Tralee] again. I told him to tell Tom [O']Connor that I was bringing all the ammo. And to pick up as many fellows as he could who had shotguns. We were joined in Castlemaine by five of the local Company (Kiltallagh, Kerry 2 Brigade), Sonnie Mason Coy. O/C, Bill Burke 1st Lieut., Mick Sullivan 2nd Lieut., Tom Knightly, and Billy Keane, who acted as chief scout and came on ahead of Tans.[11] Tom Connor arrived with about fifteen men. He had sent on word to the Hut, that we were going on with it [an ambush] ourselves.
>
> We went to the north of the village [Castlemaine] and there was no suitable position there, so we came on through the village, realising that the village was a more dangerous problem than the Tans. We knew they would stop for a drink and would be told we were out. We went on to Jack Flynn's gate and made our decision there. There were six pubs in the village, and we took the guns from twelve of our fellows and sent them [members of Fianna Éireann] to the pubs to stay there in twos until the Tans passed through.

The deployment of members of Fianna Éireann to local bars was not unusual. Police patrols regularly stopped for liquid refreshment, and drinking alcohol while on duty was particularly common among members of the Auxiliaries and Black and Tans. Mulvihill and Jack Flynn knew that on this day, one of the warmest of the summer of 1921, the thirst would get the better of the bicycle patrol as soon as they arrived in Castlemaine: at about 2 p.m. the party stopped in the village and entered Griffin's Bar for refreshment.

By this time, dozens of IRA men had assembled near Castlemaine, among them several members of the Tralee IRA who had arrived from the Hut. Remarkably, the O/C of the men at the Fybough hideaway, Paddy Cahill, stayed behind and did not participate in the ambush. Tom O'Connor of Milltown took command of those assembled, including members of the Milltown Company, the Kiltallagh Company under Alexander 'Sonny' Mason, as well as Johnny Connor from Farmers' Bridge, Dan Keating from Castlemaine (who was a member of the IRA in Tralee) and Tadhg Brosnan of Castlegregory, who was based at the Hut.

While in Castlemaine, the RIC and Black and Tans received several warnings from local civilians that the IRA had been active in the area and were planning an attack. Despite the tip-off, McCaughey and his men decided to continue on their journey along the main road, with the foolhardy commander refusing to heed advice to 'turn off my road for any Shinner'.[12] It was a display of bravado that had deadly consequences. The IRA decided to attack the patrol on a straight half-mile length of the road between Castlemaine and Milltown at the townland of Ballymacandy. It was not an obvious location for an ambush, but Mulvihill and the others decided to use this to their advantage:

> We were steeped with luck that day. We placed the fellows on the half mile straight, inside the fence, and when we had them in position ... We had not much time so we went [with] half of them to the head and half to the rear guard. Billy Keane [Fianna Éireann] arrived and told us that they [the RIC and Black and Tans] were having a consultation on the Railway Bridge. They had been told that we were ahead, but decided they were dead safe as far as Milltown, and they would branch off there as we would be waiting at Kilderry.[13] They came, bunched up and our fellows scattered. The order was – no stir until the first shot rang out ahead.

Remarkably, despite the intensity of the exchanges, there was only one IRA casualty:

> We were standing around at the western end of [the] field and Jerry Myles was just inside [the] fence when a Tan popped up and said – 'I'll have you, you bastard' and fired.[14] As he did Jerry threw himself forward and the bullet ripped his shoulder blade and ripped it open. He got up and ran along inside the fence to me and asked me to take him away. He was only half conscious. I sent four fellows for a door and mattress to Cronin's and dispatched a scout across the field to Glenellen to tell

> Doctor Sheehan to meet us at the old road, that we had a wounded man. Dr Sheehan was the Battalion Medical Officer at the time.[15] Four fellows took Jerry along and the doctor was waiting at the spot and fixed him up.

Over the course of approximately thirty minutes, five of the police party were killed or mortally wounded. The first to fall were DI McCaughey and Sgt James Collery, the father of nine children who lived in Milltown. Seriously wounded were constables John Quirke and John McCormack. Quirke was dead within an hour and McCormack succumbed to his injuries the following morning. The final killing was at the hands of Dan Mulvihill. Mulvihill had been hiding in the ditch along a narrow lane between the main road and the Great Southern and Western railway line that ran parallel with the main road. Alongside him was Bryan ('Bryannie') O'Brien of the Keel IRA.[16] Mulvihill recalled:

> The whitethorn was high and green and we could not see who was running. Bryannie Brien and [my]self were standing at the end of a bohereen. I said: 'We will not fire until he comes out in the open. It could be one of our fellows.' We saw the army pants and R.I.C tunic in front of us and that finished the fighting.

Mulvihill, perhaps unsurprisingly, does not specifically reference his shooting of the RIC man in his own memoir. In testimony given many years later, however, Bertie Scully of the

Glencar IRA stated that he loaned the gun of Joe Taylor – who was fatally wounded near Glencar the previous February – to Dan Mulvihill: 'I gave the loan of Joe's gun, a repeating shotgun, to Mulvihill, and it was with this gun the R.I.C. man ... was shot.'[17] Greg Ashe of Lispole later recounted that at the ambush Mulvihill had 'a repeating shotgun and he let lash with it'.[18]

Mulvihill's victim was Constable Joseph Cooney. A native of County Roscommon, the twenty-five-year-old had been assigned to Kerry since March 1919. He was based at Glencar before moving to Killorglin. Cooney was one of two RIC members injured during an attack on the RIC at Curraghbeg, Glencar on 16 July 1920, which forced the constabulary to abandon their barracks. He was also a member of the police party that arrested and killed Joe Taylor in February 1921. Cooney's death at Ballymacandy was witnessed by another policeman from Killorglin Barracks. Constable Patrick Bergin was with Cooney close to the front of the cycling party and stated:

> I knelt down and opened fire. After firing two shots I was myself wounded in the left leg. I fell on my face. I regained a kneeling position and I saw a man in civilian clothes firing at Constable Cooney. He had a rifle. I had a clear view of his head and shoulders. He was the width of the road from me – about 7 or 8 yards. He was dressed in a rain coat and a cap pulled down on one side of his face. I fired at him with my revolver and he ducked down behind the hedge and I saw him no more. I threw a Mill's [*sic*] bomb in his direction and then ran down the road

> towards the rear of the patrol, where I saw some of the [police] patrol putting up a fight.[19]

Cooney lay dying on the road as the local Catholic curate, a former chaplain in the British Army, Fr Alexander 'Sandy' O'Sullivan, administered the Last Rites. As he prayed with Cooney, the constable coughed and began to mumble. According to one IRA account he told Fr O'Sullivan: 'Tell the Glencar lads that it wasn't I shot Joe Taylor.'[20] Cooney, it appeared, was denying that he had fired the shots that had killed Joe Taylor months previously.

Five men lay dead or dying on the road at Ballymacandy, seven others who were either injured or had escaped being shot were fleeing to Killorglin. It would not be long before the military descended on Milltown and Castlemaine:

> We had killed five of them and wounded two, and things had got very quiet and we could not see anyone. I had gone out [onto the road] and got a service rifle, a Webley, slings of ammo. And about twenty-five rounds of .45. We gathered the stuff – we got seven rifles, six Webleys, about seven rounds of ammo for each Webley and six hundred rounds of .303. We also got their nice new bikes. The crowd split up and went their different ways. I went across the fields to my home which was about 900 yards away. I wanted to get all the stuff that was lying around dumped, as I knew that they would be told that I ran the operations, and the house would be burned ... They

> [later] told my mother they would get me. She said: 'Ye won't, if he sees ye first.'

Mulvihill 'got a change of clothes and followed the boys'. They had only one destination in mind: the safety, remoteness and familiarity of Glencar:

> I got up to them as they were about to cross the [River] Laune at Ballymalis.[21] We went right through to Breens, Gearha [in Glencar], and held him [Jerry Myles] there for the night. The following evening, we took him to the top of Glencar. We got Mary O'Brien, Ardcanaught – nurse on holidays – to come and nurse him. We stayed around for a few days to give her a hand. When Jerry started to improve, we brought a boat to Cloon Lake, and took him on the lake everyday. I had to take him if I was around. We were great friends, and I was well able to pull a boat as I had lots of practice.

Ballymacandy was one of the final engagements of the War of Independence in County Kerry. Six weeks after the ambush, the conflict finally came to an end when a Truce was agreed in July 1921. The cessation of hostilities offered Dan and Katie Mulvihill, and the men and women of the IRA and Cumann na mBan, some respite from the uncertainty, turmoil and danger of the previous two years. But the respite would be brief and the end of one battle did not mean the end of the war.

CHAPTER 6

'The truce was on, and we could not believe it'

'THE TRUCE OF GOD, as it has been so well called, has been proclaimed in Ireland' declared the editorial in the *Kerry People* newspaper of Saturday, 16 July 1921, as it welcomed news that the War of Independence had finally come to an end just a few days previously. 'God grant,' the editor, Maurice Ryle continued, 'that it may be the harbinger of an enduring peace in our long-distracted country.'

Ryle, an experienced journalist and editor, whose newspaper was the only Kerry publication to survive the reign of terror of the Black and Tans in Kerry in 1920–21, had his finger on the popular pulse. If there was one overwhelming emotion in Kerry in the days after the War of Independence ended, it was relief. For a year and a half, the county had witnessed some of the worst brutalities of the IRA war with the forces of the Crown. The cycle of killings, ambushes, burnings, assaults, raids and reprisals had taken its toll. According to a study by Eunan O'Halpin, almost 140 people died in Kerry during the conflict, with countless others maimed and injured, among them Private Joseph Cooney, who died at the hands of Dan Mulvihill on 1 June 1921.[1] But the war had impacted not just the combatants in the ranks of the IRA on the one side and the RIC, Black and Tans and Auxiliaries on the other – innocent civilians in mid-Kerry and beyond had also borne the brunt:

> Economic and commercial activity was restricted, employment was scarce, social occasions and interaction restrained. Fear, anxiety and paranoia pervaded the community. Local memory [in Milltown] holds that when a police curfew was imposed from eight o'clock in the evening, it was a requirement that a list of occupants be written and maintained on the back of the door of each home so that it could be inspected by the police in search of those on the run. Suspicious responses would see men and women corralled in the Square for questioning. The intensification of policing methods led to more viciousness against ordinary civilians. In September, the *Kerry People* reported that 'a young man in the Milltown district was tarred and a young lady a short time previous had her hair cut.' On 9 October, it reported 'a labourer recently tarred in the Milltown district has been taken away by the Crown forces.'[2]

Some civilians bore the ultimate cost of the war: indeed, it was a civilian killed on the streets of Killarney in the dying minutes of the war who holds the unfortunate claim of being the last person to be killed in the conflict. When Hannah Carey, a waitress at the Imperial Hotel in Killarney, stepped onto the street outside her hotel moments before the Truce took effect at midday on 11 July 1921, she was killed by a bullet discharged from the gun of an RIC officer passing by, a bullet he claimed was fired accidentally.[3]

Dan Mulvihill had spent many of the final weeks of the War of Independence in the peace and security of Glencar, in the aftermath of the ambush at Ballymacandy. Jerry Myles remained under the protection of the local IRA while he recovered from his injuries. While Mulvihill and his men remained in the safe houses of the parish, talk of an end to the hostilities became more and more amplified and made its way to the foothills of Carrauntoohil: 'We returned to Glencar in late June, early July [1921] and rumours started that something was happening.' However, the announcement of the Truce on 8 July 1921 – which came into effect three days later on 11 July – did not mean an end to the fighting. If anything, the three-day window before the formal cessation of hostilities offered an opportunity for the IRA to launch a series of final attacks on the representatives of British rule in Ireland. The chance for retribution was too difficult to resist. The men gathered in Glencar decided to end the war, literally and metaphorically, with a bang:

> The date of the Truce was announced, and preparations were started for two big attacks on the eve of the Truce.

> I was against it [the planned attacks] but kept my mouth shut. One was fixed for Killorglin and another [for] Castleisland. Fellows from Killarney, Kenmare, Ballymac, and Killorglin gathered in Killorglin and the rest at Castleisland. We had twenty pounds of guncotton in a mine at Killorglin. I was to take it to the barracks. We discussed the likely effects, and the question of women and children in surrounding houses, and it was called off. It would have levelled that part of the town [Killorglin]. Castleisland went ahead and Dick Shanahan and Flynn from Gortatlea were killed there.[4] The truce was on, and we could not believe it.

As post-war negotiations began in London between the President of the Irish Republic, Éamon de Valera, and the British Prime Minister, David Lloyd George, a war-weary Mulvihill returned briefly to Brackhill without fear of being apprehended. As high politics took the place of warfare, it was a time of respite for those who had been engaged in combat for a year or more. Another Kerry IRA member, Jeremiah Murphy from east Kerry, remembered how the Truce was greeted with a combination of relief and nervousness:

> The Truce brought about much needed rest for many harassed IRA men and a little relaxation was indulged in. Some who had not been home for a year were able to see their families again, for they had not been operating in their native territory. They were either too well-known,

> or the districts might have been largely pro-British, or the terrain was very unsuitable for guerrilla warfare. But the majority of the men were able to be at home most of the time and didn't suffer from the worries of the wanted men in the flying columns ... Our leaders cautioned us about undue optimism and warned that hostilities could break out again very easily.[5]

Mulvihill's comrade, Con Casey of Tralee, described a 'feeling of intense relief' and John Joe Sheehy, also of Tralee, 'a great feeling of euphoria'.[6] Another of their comrades, Mick McGlynn, remembered that 'the cessation of the fighting was a great relief. General Headquarters issued £25 to each of us. One of our senior officers, Tommy McEllistrim of Ballymacelligott, organised a five-day holiday to Ballybunion. The holiday was a smashing success.'[7]

A fortnight into the Truce, there was some sense of a return to normal life in Kerry. The *Kerry People* captured this renewed semblance of peacetime routine in the county:

> The coming of the Truce has made a complete change in the whole face of things. Business and pleasure have once more become the features of the life of the people of Tralee. The pig and cattle fairs held in Tralee this week show how easily under altered conditions this town can regain its old commercial pre-eminence. There is an air of business and bustle all around which speaks well for the quick commercial instincts of the people – their

> readiness to seize and avail of every change that time may evolve ... The spirit of peace is abroad; it is to be seen in every face and in every form of nature. Long may this state of things continue in our beloved land.[8]

In mid-Kerry, Mulvihill and the local battalions of the IRA and Cumann na mBan made the most of a welcome reprieve from the fighting. Mulvihill continued to tend to Jerry Myles in Glencar, as he recovered from his injuries sustained at Ballymacandy, and with his comrades, enjoyed the peace and quiet of rural south Kerry:

> It was beautiful at that period. The long hot summer, the lake with boats on it. The surroundings of beech, birch, hazel and oak set it apart. It [the Caragh River] is the number one river in Ireland for fresh pearl oysters, and for years an English man came there, and with a boat, telescope and [some] sort of tongs, made a good holiday out of it; never got anything but pearls but I was with Bertie Scully when he found one for which he got 30 pounds.

The IRA had spent months interfering with transport and communication by cutting roads, smashing train lines, raiding trains and disrupting postal services and deliveries, but in the days after the Truce there were indications that those services were returning to normal too. In his diary, Major Leeson-Marshall of Callinafercy noted that the trains were operational again for the first time in three months: 'Trains ran again. Off since April 29th – about 12 weeks & post for 1st time since May 25th – 8 weeks. 72 mailbags in Milltown PO [Post Office]. Post-mistress says she can't deal with more than 5 a day. Warned her to hurry up.'[9]

A fortnight later, however, the major noticed more ominous activity when he 'met 2 processions of cars full of young men bound to the west, heard afterwards to "Hd Qts" [Headquarters] Glencar, hope it is to approve of peace being negotiated.'[10] The major's sister, Edith, Lady Gordon, who lived at Ard na Sídhe near Caragh Lake and close to the parish of Glencar, noticed plenty of similar action: the IRA, she recorded in her memoir, 'promptly made use of it [the Truce] to gather up fresh force and material for the eventual renewal of the struggle'.[11] Over the summer, she observed plenty of activity in remoter parts of south Kerry:

> In the dead of night, carts rattling suggestively could be heard going up the mountain road. Stories of prodigious armaments were whispered round. 'The biggest gun the world has ever seen' had arrived in Glencar ... My only hope was that, on its way, it would not lay Carrantuohill flat ... Several weeks passed; affairs remained some time still in the balance; nobody seemed particularly hopeful of a successful settlement.[12]

The men heading to their headquarters in Glencar were those like Mulvihill who began to use the Truce not just to rest and recover from months of combat but also to regroup and retrain in anticipation of a possible resumption of hostilities if the talks in London broke down. 'We had a Brigade training camp in Glencar, end of July [1921],' noted Mulvihill as his work with the IRA entered a new phase. In the summer of 1921, and despite the toll of the war, the IRA in Kerry was organisationally stronger and more prepared for battle than at any time during the conflict itself, due, for the most part, to an influx of new volunteers, a phenomenon which continued after the Truce. A reinvigorated IRA, buoyed by having forced the British government to the negotiating table, experienced an influx of many new recruits who, now realising that an independent Ireland was a possibility, joined the ranks in anticipation of careers in the new polity. The 'Trucileers' as they were derogatively called by those who had taken part in the war against the Black and Tans, swelled the ranks of the force to about 70,000 by the end of 1921.[13] Sinéad Joy details an increase in the ranks in places like Dingle, Ballymacelligott and Killarney.[14] Within Mulvihill's battalion, the ranks expanded and in the Callinafercy Company, for example, which encompassed a relatively small rural area between Milltown and Killorglin, there were 110 members in the summer of 1921.[15] According to Bertie Scully, the local IRA companies were in a strong position when the war came to an end:

> Kerry No. 1 Brigade was actually turned up [*sic*] to fight when the Truce came. We had the strongest Bn [Battalion] and our company was the best company. 6 [*sic*] Cos [Companies]: Glenbeigh, Glencar, Killorglin,

> Milltown, Callinafercy, Caragh Lake, Kilgobnet (toward the Gap [of Dunloe]). We had 9–10 R [rifles] and we were supplied with shotguns. We had plenty of shot. I had 900 rounds ...[16]

The release of some prisoners in the weeks and months after the Truce also provided the IRA with a morale boost and an organisational fillip. Among those released was Mulvihill's comrade, Aeneas Langford of Callinafercy, who arrived home after completing a six-month stint in prison in Spike Island and Cork Gaol: 'He was met at the [Milltown] station by the local Volunteers,' reported *The Cork Examiner*, 'who accorded him a hearty welcome, and conveyed him to his home, about two miles distant'.[17] Also released in August 1921 were TDs James Crowley of Listowel, who had been elected MP for North Kerry in 1918, and Fionán Lynch of Waterville, who had been returned for Sinn Féin in South Kerry.[18] Lynch would join the secretariat of the Irish delegation that negotiated the Anglo-Irish Treaty in London a few months later.[19]

Despite slow and steady progress in the political discussions – de Valera and Kerry TD Austin Stack met Lloyd George in London in July – the IRA's official newspaper, *An t-Óglach*, warned volunteers, on the announcement of the Truce, of the 'paramount importance of keeping their discipline, efficiency and being organised, unimpaired, during the suspension of hostilities'.[20] There remained every likelihood, if talks between the Irish and British negotiators did not succeed, of a resumption of war, with perhaps even greater intensity. A series of articles tutoring IRA foot-soldiers in various skills and techniques of warfare were published in the same newspaper over the summer and autumn with a reminder of the 'great responsibility' which lay on the IRA 'at this fateful moment in our country's history'.[21] Those tutorials were complemented by a series of training camps which sprang up across the country. Mulvihill noted a surge in drilling and training in the summer of 1921:

> I found a report giving the figure as 38,000 men, who had gone through Training Camp in the First Southern [Division]. I know that 800 men paraded at Glencar the day of the closing of the Brigade Training Camp. The 800 were from Sixth Battalion alone. The Camp had been at Lickeen House ...

Cumann na mBan members were particularly active in facilitating and catering for the camps. Annie O'Connor in Tralee 'took charge of Ashill [Ash Hill] and Chutehall IRA training camps, it was my Cumann na mBan branch that kept those camps supplied with food, clothing, bed clothes etc from funds created by [our] own efforts'.[22] Use was made of the Hut at Fybough, where IRA members trained for a fortnight.[23] At Castlegregory, volunteers were trained in 'bomb-throwing' and ambushing techniques.[24] The Ballymacelligott Company studied rifle practice, engineering and signalling, while a large training camp at Aghadoe was addressed by the Kerry TD Piaras Béaslaí.[25]

Daniel (Dan) Mulvihill. (Courtesy of Kilmainham Gaol Museum, KMGLM.20PC-1A26-22)

The SS *Aidan*, on which Mulvihill worked as a telegraphist during 1916.

The Milltown Volunteers, which Mulvihill joined in 1916.

Members of the Royal Irish Constabulary in Milltown, who were attacked by Mulvihill and the IRA in 1920 and 1921.

James (Jimmy) Cronin of the Milltown IRA and his sister Annie ('Sis'), a member of Milltown Cumann na mBan.

Tom O'Connor, officer commanding, Milltown IRA.

John (Jack) Flynn of the Milltown IRA.

Paddy Cahill, officer commanding, Kerry No. 1 Brigade IRA.

General Liam Lynch, chief of staff of the IRA during the Civil War. Mulvihill was Lynch's aide-de-camp and Lynch appointed him adjutant of the Kerry Command of the IRA in 1922. (Courtesy of Cork Public Museum)

The Hibernian Hotel in Killarney where Mulvihill was based as liaison officer during the Truce.

Óglaiġ na h-Éireann. P64/7(1)

~~Árd Oifig, Áth Cliath.~~ General Headquarters, Dublin.

Department Chief Liaison Office.

Reference No ....

GRESHAM HOTEL.

31st October, 1921.

TO:

Liaison Officer.

County: Kerry

A Chara,

I enclose you herewith your appointment as Liaison Officer for the County of Kerry

You will take up duties at once.

The British County Inspector has been notified of your appointment and you should get into touch with him immediately.

Where an Office address has not yet been notified to me you should do so without delay.

Do Chara,

Fintan Murphy Comdt

act CHIEF LIAISON OFFICER.

Mulvihill's letter of appointment as liaison officer in 1921. (Courtesy of UCD Archives)

He reported to General Emmet Dalton, senior liaison officer in Dublin. (Courtesy of the National Library of Ireland)

The anti-Treaty IRA convention at the Mansion House in Dublin on 9 April 1922. Mulvihill is pictured in the fourth row. (Courtesy of Kilmainham Gaol Museum, KMGLM.20PC-1A26-22)

'The best soldier I ever knew'. Con O'Leary of Kerry No. 2 Brigade. (Courtesy of Kilmainham Gaol Museum, KMGLM.20PC-1A26-22)

Hut No. 17.

James Brennan, Thomas Cassidy, Patrick Durnin, John Doggett, James Davidson, Patrick Dolan, Patrick Farrell, Robert Fitzgerald, James Fox, Patrick, Fitzgerald, Patrick Farrelley, Michael Flannery, John Flaherty, Patrick Finn, Gerald Fitzgerald, Patrick Garband, Michael Gaynor, William Ganby, Peter Griffin, Joseph Gaynor, John Goldrick, Martin Gordon, James Gibbons, Vincent Gogan, James Harkin, Sean Hayes, Patrick Halley, Christie McNally, James McGrath, Thomas Murray, Patrick McGowan, Owen McFadden, William O'Leary, James O'Connor, John O'Rourke, Charles O'Reilly, Frank Stack, Martin Slattery, Patrick Sweeney, Hugh Stynes, James Sherlock, James Spellman, Hugh Smith, Christie Smith, George Thompson, James Rigney, Sean Reidy, Matthew Ryan, Patrick Clarke, Michael Flaherty, Patrick Dorley, George Owens, Percy Whelan, Charles Myles, John Fitzpatrick, John King, Thomas Brennan, Timothy Healy, Richard Egan, Daniel Mulvihill, Martin McGrath, Michael O'Leary.

(Two off hunger-strike.)

Report from *Éire*, which lists Mulvihill as one of those on hunger strike in 1923.

Mulvihill's passport photograph from 1925. (Courtesy of UCD Archives)

Patrick 'Paudeen' O'Keeffe, deputy governor of Mountjoy Prison while Mulvihill was interned there in 1923.

Mulvihill (back, centre) pictured at the handover of Spike Island in 1938. Taoiseach Éamon de Valera (middle, left) is pictured with other ministers, including Frank Aiken, James Ryan and P.J. Ruttledge. (Courtesy of the Mulvihill family)

One Man's Ireland 1975 Skeleton only

This is written from memory, after well over fifty years. It of course contains an amount of mistakes. The main facts are all correct, but as it is a personal account, and of course personal experience, it will not always agree with what other people saw. I will try as far as possible to avoid anything that would be contrversial.

I went to London on I think the I2th April I9I6, and stood a Test as a Learner in Marconi House. the following day. I got through, and worked there. I got seventeen and six per week as Learner, and paid fifteen Shillings for my Digs in Praed Street, across from St Marys Hospital. We were trained in the Under ground portion, as were the Air Core, and the Marines. We worked hard there, and three evenings a week went back from seven to nine. We made friends in the most unlikely places, one of mine was a Ginger haired Canadian. I used to go out to Stagg Lane, it was as far as I remember a Training ground, and I flew in a Plane with him. A one far removed from the ones today, it was a Biplane I'd say it was all timber ,cloth ,and wicker work. Maximum speed about eighty miles per hour. I spent most of my off time in Hyde Park, reading any Science Ficti I could get hold of. George Griffith. H.G.Wells. Jules Verne. What changes in sixty years.

Extract from an original copy of Mulvihill's memoir. It includes a handwritten title, *One Man's Ireland*, and was a first draft or 'skeleton only'.

Florence O'Donoghue, pictured in 1964. (Courtesy of the National Library of Ireland)

Mulvihill pictured in the 1970s.

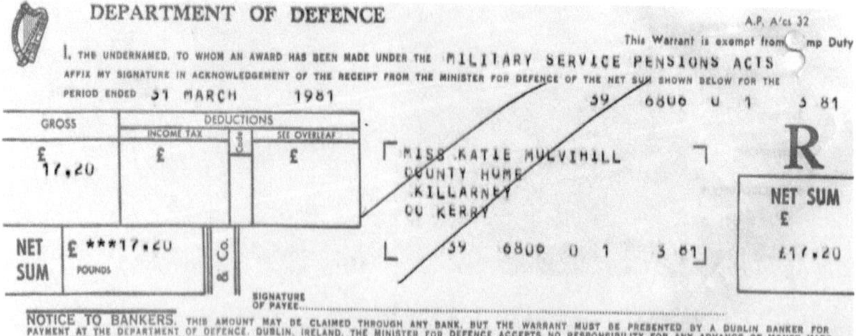

DEPARTMENT OF DEFENCE

A.P. A/cs 32

This Warrant is exempt from Stamp Duty

I, THE UNDERNAMED, TO WHOM AN AWARD HAS BEEN MADE UNDER THE MILITARY SERVICE PENSIONS ACTS AFFIX MY SIGNATURE IN ACKNOWLEDGEMENT OF THE RECEIPT FROM THE MINISTER FOR DEFENCE OF THE NET SUM SHOWN BELOW FOR THE PERIOD ENDED 31 MARCH 1981

39 6806 0 1 3 81

GROSS	DEDUCTIONS: INCOME TAX	Code	SEE OVERLEAF
£ 17.20	£		£

MISS KATIE MULVIHILL
COUNTY HOME
KILLARNEY
CO KERRY

39 6806 0 1 3 81

R

NET SUM £ ***17.20 POUNDS

NET SUM £ 17.20

SIGNATURE OF PAYEE

NOTICE TO BANKERS. THIS AMOUNT MAY BE CLAIMED THROUGH ANY BANK, BUT THE WARRANT MUST BE PRESENTED BY A DUBLIN BANKER FOR PAYMENT AT THE DEPARTMENT OF DEFENCE, DUBLIN, IRELAND. THE MINISTER FOR DEFENCE ACCEPTS NO RESPONSIBILITY FOR ANY ADVANCE OF MONEY MADE AGAINST THE WARRANT IN ANTICIPATION OF ITS ACCEPTANCE IN THE DEPARTMENT OF DEFENCE.

Katie Mulvihill's pension cheque, which was cancelled on her death in 1981. **(Courtesy of the Military Archives, Katie Mulvihill MSPC/ MSP34REF31270/34E6806)**

Closer to home for Mulvihill, in Milltown the IRA established a base and a training camp at Kilburn House, a short distance from the village. Dating from the 1730s, the house and gardens were shrouded by large beech, chestnut and oak trees, offering good cover under which to hold a camp.[26] While the IRA drilled and maintained their weapons, they were catered for by local Cumann na mBan members, such as Annie Cronin and Katie Mulvihill. Katie also acted as a minder of money for the Milltown IRA at this time, and when the Truce was declared she handed over £350 – the equivalent of almost £20,000 today – to the company quartermaster to 'buy arms in England'.[27] If there was to be a return to war, the local IRA and Cumann na mBan were amassing the necessary guns and ammunition and training their personnel to carry on the fight.

+++

Preparations for the resumption of the conflict were not without hazard, however: in October 1921 Mulvihill lost one of his closest friends and allies in a tragic accident. Maurice (Mossie) Casey from Ballinoe lived a short distance from the Mulvihills at Brackhill. Along with his brother, Michael, he was 'into everything' the IRA was involved in locally during the War of Independence: Mulvihill described the pair as 'two great willing workers'.[28] The Caseys were steeped in republican activism. Their sister, Mary, was in the Firies Company of Cumann na mBan, spending much time 'seeing after the wants of members of the Flying Columns'.[29]

On 22 October Casey and Mulvihill and five others were making 'black powder' in a shed at Molahiffe near Firies, a few miles from Castlemaine. The making of gunpowder for bullets and explosives was 'a hazardous process'.[30] The gunpowder ignited and Casey was badly scalded while another volunteer, Denis Coffey from Farranfore, was seriously injured in the hand.[31] A third man, Denis Rahilly, was blown through the roof of the shed but survived. Remarkably, Mulvihill was not injured in the blast. Casey, then just twenty-four years old, was taken to a nearby house but was in a serious condition. He was removed to the infirmary in Tralee where he succumbed to his injuries – including shock and 'burns all over his body' – five days later.[32] 'All [his] face and hands burned away.'[33] Mulvihill does not record his reaction to his friend's agonising death nor the effect it had on him and the Milltown Company of the IRA. However, the death neither deterred nor prevented him and his comrades from remaining active members of the IRA, despite the near and present dangers which prevailed. It was a grim reminder to Mulvihill and all his comrades that though the guns had fallen silent, the prospect of death was never far away.

CHAPTER 7

'Things are getting worse every day'

DAN MULVIHILL'S TIME IN Glencar during the Truce in the summer of 1921 was to be short-lived. His IRA superiors had an important role in mind for the battle-hardened twenty-four-year-old. The end of the War of Independence in July had created something of a legal, political and military vacuum, with potential for chaos and disorder while the future governance of Ireland remained uncertain. The British government and its forces remained in control of the country, but that control was precarious as the constitutional future of Ireland was ironed out during discussions in Downing Street, and some degree of compromise was inevitable. While the negotiations – which eventually led to the Anglo-Irish Treaty of December 1921 – were underway in London, both sides of the conflict in Ireland recognised the potential for trouble from combatants and civilians alike who might try to avail of the political vacuum to commit crimes, settle old scores and take advantage of the uncertainty and instability. In essence, there was the potential for a continuation of the War of Independence in all but name. Despite their mutual loathing, both the republicans and the Crown forces recognised the need to maintain peace and, if necessary, punish those who subverted it.

Key to ensuring that peace and order were maintained during the Truce, while the politicians tussled with each other over a legal and political settlement, was agreement between the IRA and their opponents that order would be preserved through communication, collaboration and cooperation. The British Army and the leaders of the Dáil agreed to a series of commitments to ensure that law and order were maintained while the constitutional question was being settled. For the British, a series of commitments were put forward by General Nevil Macready on behalf of the Crown forces. They agreed that from 11 July 1921, when the Truce took effect, there would be:

1. No incoming troops, Royal Irish Constabulary (RIC), auxiliary police and munitions. No movements for military purposes of troops and munitions, except maintenance drafts.
2. No provocative display of forces – armed or unarmed.
3. It is understood that all provisions of this Truce apply to the martial law area equally with the rest of Ireland.
4. No pursuit of Irish officers or men or war material or military stores.

5. No secret agents, noting description or movements, and no interference with the movements of Irish persons, military or civil, and no attempts to discover the haunts or habits of Irish officers and men.
6. No pursuit or observance of lines of communication or connection.[1]

For the Irish political and military leaders, the commitments were given by Robert Barton TD and Eamonn Duggan TD, who agreed as follows:

1. Attacks on Crown forces and civilians to cease.
2. No provocative displays of forces, armed or unarmed.
3. No interference with Government or private property.
4. To discountenance and prevent any action likely to cause disturbance of the peace which might necessitate military interference.[2]

In such a very febrile and politically delicate situation, these commitments were ambitious. But how to ensure the terms were observed and how to police the implementation of the agreement? The solution, rather innovatively and despite the post-war tensions between both sides, was to jointly oversee and regulate the Truce terms. A system was devised whereby alleged breaches of the Truce would be shared and investigated and a report prepared. Where an IRA representative believed that a breach of the terms occurred, it would be taken up with the local RIC or army officer and vice versa. The post of chief liaison officer was established to ensure close communication and oversight of the system between the British and the Irish, with Brigadier General J.E.S. Brind assuming the role for the British forces and Eamonn Duggan (one of the plenipotentiaries who would sign the Anglo-Irish Treaty in December 1921) for the Provisional Government and the IRA. They oversaw a network of local liaison officers who were assigned to cover a county or similarly large territory. That sworn enemies who had, until very recently, been fighting each other in an increasingly brutal and bloody conflict, agreed and managed to sustain this system for several months was remarkable. As Mark Duncan explains:

> Rather than rush to arrest and risk inflaming matters, it was to these Sinn Féin [liaison] officers that RIC constables were instructed to consult in the event of obvious local breaches of the truce terms ... Although not without strain or occasional rancour, the system of appointing liaison officers to ensure the oversight and smooth operation of the truce did work.[3]

In the late summer of 1921, Dan Mulvihill received an order to come to Dublin. Liam Lynch, O/C of the 1st Southern Division of the IRA, wanted to see him:

> Sometime in August [1921], I went to Brigade H.Q. and later on Liam Lynch appointed me as Liaison Officer for Kerry. I went to Dublin and was commissioned with a

> whole lot of fellows from different counties. I set up in the Hibernian Hotel, Killarney (one of our own). I liked the job. I had a sense of humour then. I was the link between our fellows and the British Forces, and knowing them, and how they looked on us, it was good fun. The [army] heads varied, some of them decent, some ex-officers with swelled heads who regarded us as savages. On the British side were heads of different army posts in the county:.the R.I.C., Black and Tans and the Auxiliaries.

Mulvihill lost no time in embracing his new role, for which he received a payment of £5 per week.[4] He was provided with an office at the Hibernian Hotel on New Street in Killarney. The hotel was conveniently located across the street from the post office, to which Mulvihill would be a regular visitor in subsequent months, sending reports to Dublin. He was formally appointed to the role on 31 October 1921.[5] His principal point of contact on the British side was RIC captain Frederick George Lancaster, as well as other senior officers in the constabulary and the army. Lancaster was a native of Epsom in Surrey and was a police officer in England before joining the West Yorkshire Regiment of the British Army at the beginning of the First World War. After the war, he was posted to Ireland as a district inspector with the RIC, based in Killarney. In May 1921 he had been wounded when a police vehicle crashed into a trench cut in the road at Ballymalis between Killarney and Killorglin, for which he was later awarded £300 in compensation.[6] Mulvihill recounted his own impressions of Captain Lancaster:

> On the British side, I dealt with the R.I.C. (the County Inspector and about eight superintendents), the Army [in] Tralee, Killarney, Kenmare and Valentia. The army crowd were alright: they wanted to be left in peace and carry [on] their day. The R.I.C., with about two or three exceptions, were always looking for something to kick about. They had been for so long 'Cock of the Walk', they couldn't conform. I knew a Captain Lancaster – a brave man – superintendent in Killarney, ex-British Army, a career man. He was a pain in the neck, always looking for something to make off about. He had a few sergeants in barracks who were frightened of their [*sic*; his] like: that he would get them all killed. Our fellows [the IRA] had no intention of touching them. Of course, there is always the blackguard in any crowd who can start trouble, especially if he gets a few fellows half drunk.

Alleged IRA crimes or misdemeanours, which were believed to be in contravention of the terms of the Truce, were usually reported by Lancaster in writing to Mulvihill and were often addressed to the 'S.F. [Sinn Féin] Liaison Officer'. Mulvihill would be required to investigate alleged offences by referring the matter to local IRA brigade leaders or any other appropriate local IRA commander: 'I dealt with "Free" [Humphrey] Murphy, John Joe [J.J.] Rice and Jeremiah Reardon on the I.R.A side.' Murphy, Rice and Reardon (or Riordan) were the IRA commanders in Kerry Brigade Nos 1, 2 and 3 respectively. The local commander would, in turn, be obliged to present details and any intelligence to Mulvihill. Vice versa, alleged misbehaviour by his members would be relayed to Lancaster for investigation. The cumulative effort was designed to maintain peace and to warn the perpetrators that breaches of the Truce would not be tolerated.

As well as reports from Lancaster and his peers, complaints about incidents in Kerry were often lodged directly with the Chief Liaison Officer, Eamonn Duggan, who was based at the Gresham Hotel in Dublin. If the matter related to Kerry, it would be sent to Mulvihill in Killarney with an instruction to carry out a thorough investigation: 'Breaches of the Truce could mean anything, and most of the reports came from Dublin for a start. When reports arrived, they just put them into an envelope and sent them to [the] county concerned with a note: "Please investigate and report."'

For most of this period, Mulvihill's point of contact in Dublin was Emmet Dalton, one of the senior liaison officers who worked with Duggan. The American-born Dalton had fought in the trenches on the Western Front during the First World War but joined the IRA before the War of Independence began. He would forever be synonymous with the most pivotal moment of the Civil War that followed the Truce, during which time he was an officer in the National Army. Mulvihill recalled:

> Emmet Dalton was acting as Head Liaison Officer.[7] He was the fellow who drove the Armoured Car into Mountjoy in the attempt to rescue Sean Mac Eoin.[8] He was the man who was in the car with Michael Collins

> at Béal na Bláth, where Collins met his death. Emmet was an ex-British Officer. I think he worked for Metro Goldwyn Mayer too. His daughter, Audrey, was a film star, she got married and chucked the films. The last picture I saw her in was *Girls of Pleasure Island*.

+++

Mulvihill may have considered the role of liaison officer to be 'good fun' for much of this time, but, if his official papers from this period of his life are anything to go by, it was an extremely busy, tense and turbulent one. Most of Mulvihill's correspondence and documents from his time as liaison officer for Kerry survive and are held in the archives of University College Dublin.[9] As a collection of archives of one such liaison officer specific to one county at this particular time, they offer unique insights into a period of significant political tension in Ireland, and provide a fascinating glimpse into the function of individuals who had a critical role in maintaining the Truce and ensuring that law and order prevailed. Moreover, they ensure that the Truce period – between the end of the War of Independence and the departure of British forces from most of the country during 1922 – which has often been neglected because of a focus on the wars which bookend it, can be illuminated in substantial detail.

While Mulvihill delegated many of the investigations of alleged breaches of the Truce to the local brigade leader, he was often required to travel to different parts of the county to carry out his own investigations. Ironically, on one occasion, Mulvihill's journey to west Kerry to investigate such a matter was hampered by the damage to roads that had been carried out by the IRA to stymie the movements of the Crown forces:

> My first investigation concerned a Coast Guard Station out on the tip of the Dingle Peninsula. It had been burned.[10] I got a wire to go and investigate. I got 'Honey' Donoghue with a new car, and we left Killarney for Tralee in the morning and, trenches [in the roads] being still open – around November 1st, 1921 – we got to Dingle late that night.

Coastguard stations, as strategically important defence posts for the British Army and Navy, were a particular target for IRA members who chose to ignore the terms of the ceasefire: in November 1921 Mulvihill was asked to examine why the IRA had broken into and seized the coastguard base at Lackee Point near Sneem the moment it had been evacuated by British forces.[11]

Many of the early complaints and allegations of wrongdoing that found their way to Mulvihill's desk in Killarney emanated from what he dubbed 'the upper crust' or the landowning Anglo-Irish gentry, many of whose homes had been looted, attacked or taken over by the IRA during and after the War of Independence. Across Kerry, several of the so-called 'big houses' had been IRA targets, not only for use as training camps because of the accommodation and facilities they provided but also for arson and robbery. The houses were considered a vestige of British rule and of a Protestant ascendancy, but the attacks were often rooted in land agitation and local grievances.[12] Mulvihill was involved in investigating several issues relating to the homes of the Anglo-Irish gentry in Kerry: 'The first breaches of [the] Truce were all from the upper crust, who had big houses lying idle. They were all taken over by the I.R.A. as Training Camps – Aghadoe House, Metropole Hotel, Victoria Hotel, Barrow House, Valentia, Waterville, Dooks, Castlegregory, Dromore, Colonel Warden's and about a score of others in north and south Kerry.'

Colonel Charles Wallace Warden's property in south Kerry, Derryquin Castle, now the Parknasilla Hotel, was a regular target for the IRA, with incidents on the large estate 'occurring day after day' and these cases dominate Mulvihill's files from this period.[13] Warden was a particularly loathed landlord, and civilians and the IRA took advantage of the War of Independence and the months which followed to seize land, steal property and terrorise Warden and his family. This would culminate in the castle being burned in October 1922 during the Civil War.[14] Mulvihill was asked to investigate why the castle had been raided 'on nineteen occasions' since the Truce.[15] The response from his comrades in the IRA was illustrative of the residual tensions after the war and the way in which such complaints were often dismissed. An adjutant with the Kerry No. 2 Brigade advised Mulvihill that in many cases, 'you could hardly call them raids as he [Warden] was always politely asked for everything that was taken'. The adjutant could not promise that the local IRA would prevent civilians from trespassing on the Derryquin estate, noting their revulsion for Warden as 'one of the old landlord types'.[16]

Another wealthy landowner who was the subject of IRA intimidation and robbery during Mulvihill's tenure as liaison officer was Major Arthur Blennerhassett of Ballyseedy near Tralee. So perturbed was Blennerhassett by the extent of damage and theft on his estate that he visited Emmet Dalton at the office of the chief liaison officer in Dublin at the beginning of 1922. Their discussion prompted an angry missive from Dalton to Mulvihill in Killarney:

> Major Blennerhassett, Ballyseedy, Tralee has been in with me. He does not strike me as a man given to untruths. The affair he told me about is truly amazing. I believe that since the truce he lost about 5 in-calf heifers, 20 Lincoln ewes, 10 Lincoln yearlings, 50 trees were cut and taken away on two different days. The demesne was broken down, and stones carted away. This if true is truly outrageous, and it would be ridiculous if the perpetrators could not be traced ... The fact that the Major is a Unionist and has never been much of a friend of ours, should not prejudice the case.[17]

Civilians who were perceived to be close to the British authorities and the military received little quarter from the IRA when complaints were made to Mulvihill and others in liaison roles. A Miss Dunkin, who was described as 'an alien, being

Scotch', was reported to Mulvihill as 'habitually entertaining Crown Forces at her house and supplying them with any little information she had to give', but whether Dunkin met with any punishment as a result is not recorded.[18]

+++

Many of Mulvihill's files from the Truce period relate to the impact of the so-called Belfast Boycott. The boycott of goods and produce from Belfast resulted from the expulsion of many Catholic workers from their jobs in the city's shipyards and other employments, and a cycle of sectarian violence in Northern Ireland in the summer of 1920. Dáil Éireann reacted by imposing a boycott on goods from Belfast. Products believed to be manufactured in or emanating from the city were seized from trains by the IRA to prevent them from getting to market. 'Under the Belfast Boycott,' Mulvihill wrote, 'stuff belonging to Belfast firms was taken off train [*sic*] and at the railway stations.' Mulvihill was asked by the RIC district inspector in Listowel to investigate one such episode: the district inspector alleged that the goods porter at the local railway station was held at gunpoint while armed and masked men 'destroyed 5 cases of tobacco, consigned to local traders from the firm of Messrs Clarke Ltd., of Dublin, Belfast and Limerick'.[19] Also in Kerry, goods 'from England' destined for local retailers or suppliers were regularly seized by the IRA. In many instances, the number of items seized was small in size and quantity: Captain Lancaster was particularly exercised by the theft of 'six boxes of floor polish and disinfectant', which were to be delivered to merchants in Killorglin and the receipts for which were signed by the IRA, as well as 'blacklisted English farm goods' taken from the train in Farranfore.[20]

Lancaster was detailed in his appeals to Mulvihill for answers about raids that he alleged were carried out on the railways and which he contended were provocative and in contravention of the terms of the Truce as agreed. The details of the items seized highlights the significant wider impact of the boycott on the local military, the wider civilian population and local businesses. A list prepared by Lancaster on St Stephen's Day 1921, of items recently taken by 'IRA men' from a stalled train at Ballybrack railway station, was a case in point:

> 17 Boxes Foodstuffs Army and Navy Canteen, Tralee
> 1 Cask Foodstuffs Army and Navy Canteen, Tralee
> 1 Crate Cheese Army and Navy Canteen, Tralee
> 3 Bags Vegetables Army and Navy Canteen, Tralee
> 1 Cardboard Box Army and Navy Canteen, Tralee
> 1 Pcl [Parcel] Drapery, Munster Warehouse, Tralee
> 3 Bags Sugar for Mr Casey, Lispoole [*sic*]
> 1 Pcl Boots for Messrs Hilliard, Tralee
> 1 Box Tobacco for Mr Sullivan, Tralee
> 1 Box Drapery goods for Mr O'Leary, Tralee
> 3 Pcl Drapery Goods for Messrs Revington, Tralee[21]

Mulvihill became increasingly perturbed by the extent of the seizure of goods in this way and was concerned about the consequences. He was moved to warn the Kerry IRA brigades that such items should be returned:

> All the goods taken so far will have to be handed back at once unless you have an order from H.Q. authorising the taking of them ... most of the stuff has been taken by our [Republican] police and I am sure there is other stuff being taken in their name. If it is allowed to continue it will mean a wholesale sweep [of the area by British forces] some day soon.[22]

Mulvihill was also acutely conscious of the reputational damage and the negative propaganda that would arise from breaches of the Truce by IRA members or their failure to adequately investigate and prevent any subversion of its terms. In one message to the Kerry No. 3 Brigade, which was based in the Cahersiveen area in south Kerry, Mulvihill warned that the intimidation of a local postman, whose mailbag was repeatedly checked by IRA men, was counterproductive: 'This is the second time he has been held up within the past week. Could you arrange to stop it, as the police are laughing at the way things are going. They [the IRA] have no control over their men.'[23]

The Mulvihill Papers also highlight the way in which civilians used the political and legal vacuum to engage in criminal activity and petty theft. In many such instances, the IRA was accused of, or assumed to have been responsible for, various incidents. In one such case, a warning notice and signal lamp were stolen from the railway line near Castleisland, but the local company reported that this was 'a case of common theft'.[24] Mulvihill also dealt with the more mundane matter of stolen bicycles: in November 1921 John Murray of Coologues, Kilgarvan, implored Mulvihill to assist in the return of bicycles stolen by 'the Volunteers of Kilgarvan', which prevented him from being able to travel to cattle fairs.[25] Unfortunately Mulvihill was unable to help, as the bicycles had been taken 'prior to the Truce'.[26]

+++

The signing of the Treaty on 6 December 1921 had an immediate effect on the unity and cohesion within the ranks of the IRA and elsewhere. Its terms – signed just five months after the end of the War of Independence – meant that the new Irish Free State would have Dominion status and remain part of the British Commonwealth, Ireland would have a governor general, and perhaps most controversially, members of the Irish Parliament would be required to swear an oath of allegiance to the British monarch. Politically, in Kerry, the six TDs for the constituency divided equally when it came to a vote for or against the Treaty in the Dáil, with three – Fionán Lynch, Piaras Béaslaí and James Crowley – voting in favour and three – Paddy Cahill, Thomas O'Donoghue and Austin Stack – voting against. The pact was endorsed by the Dáil by a narrow majority of just seven votes. Within the Sinn Féin party and the ranks of IRA and Cumann na mBan ruptures began to develop quickly, with pro- and anti-Treaty camps emerging in all three organisations.

As the political temperature increased and as the divisions over the Treaty became more apparent, there was a notable increase in IRA attacks on the British forces in Kerry, which were led particularly by those who were hostile to the Treaty. Those anti-Treaty volunteers not only considered the supporters of the Treaty to be traitors, they also believed that the Provisional Government and the signatories to the pact were operating hand in glove with the British political and military establishment in failing to secure an Irish republic. The military in Kerry was increasingly targeted by anti-Treaty IRA companies in various parts of the county. In the middle of January 1922, for example, Mulvihill was presented with a long list of incidents involving attacks on the police and the army, including the theft of a Crossley Tender in Tralee, shots being fired at five soldiers on patrol by '15 armed men', the kidnapping of two soldiers 'at Tralee station' on 12 January and other interference with the work of the military.[27] Individual members of the Crown forces were often singled out for attack by a more audacious IRA and their civilian supporters, who assumed that their actions would have few, if any, consequences amid the political instability. An RIC constable wrote to Mulvihill about his ordeal when he was set upon by 'about thirty men' while he was walking to James O'Sullivan's public house in Brosna:

> One of them gave me a blow on the face and the other struck me with some instrument on the back of the head. I was then knocked to the ground and as many of the men who could get at me kicked me. After some

> time, I shouted 'I'm done, I'm done.' I feigned death and the crowd then left me. As they were going away, one of them said 'we'll have the little bastard again in the morning.' A revolver shot was then fired and the crowd shouted 'Up the I.R.A.'[28]

An incident involving Mulvihill's old nemesis, Head Constable Blake of the Killorglin RIC, was reported to the Hibernian Hotel. Mulvihill and members of his battalion had, as detailed in Chapter Four, attempted to kill Blake at his home in February 1921, but the attempt had been aborted. Blake was accosted on the platform at Killorglin railway station on 11 November 1921 by two men, Patrick O'Shea and John Riordan, who were 'evidently acting as S.F. police'. They insisted that the head constable pay rates, which they claimed were due to the local republican court, and boarded the train with him and continued to harangue him during the journey.[29]

The involvement of the 'S.F. police' in the Blake episode highlights how the republicans' own courts and policing regime continued after the War of Independence had ended. The Irish Republican Police (IRP) had been set up in the spring of 1920 to undermine the British administration of justice in Ireland and to subvert the police. The IRP ensured that the judgements of the Republican Courts – or the Dáil Courts – which were set up by Dáil Éireann in June 1920, were upheld and implemented. In one instance, Mulvihill's attention was drawn by the RIC to an effort by the IRP in Cahersiveen to prevent a local woman from entering the Cahersiveen Quarter Sessions (district courts which were still under British administration) to sue for a decree for possession of a house. He was warned to 'arrange that Mrs. O'Regan be assured there will be no repetition of this interference with her liberty'.[30]

The audacity and fearlessness of some in the IRA and the IRP were also apparent in material that crossed Mulvihill's desk in the form of other allegations: in November 1921 he was asked to probe why a 'large number of civilians' were 'openly carrying arms' in Kilgarvan village in a 'direct breach of the Truce'.[31] But those among the British military could be equally daring: the following month, the business premises of Patrick O'Driscoll in Knightstown on Valentia Island was attacked by 'big marines, about six in number', during which his wife was injured and the doors and windows smashed.[32]

The beginning of 1922 brought an increasing urgency, impatience and sometimes anger to correspondence to Mulvihill from the British forces and from the staff of the office of the chief liaison officer in Dublin. Continued attacks on civilians, such as Colonel Warden at Derryquin, were labelled 'most outrageous', and demands to 'put an end to it' were manifold.[33] There were warnings of the introduction of martial law if the security situation deteriorated further amid what Mulvihill dubbed 'a fresh wave of crime' in the county in the weeks after the Treaty was signed.[34] The increase in violence and disturbance was exemplified by the shooting dead by Crown forces in January 1922 of Patrick (Percy) Hannafin, a young member of Fianna Éireann, during an attempt to seize an army vehicle from a garage on Edward Street in Tralee. Another volunteer, Michael

Mullaly, was badly wounded. The response of the local Black and Tans was swift and furious as Mulvihill recalled. It prompted the customary rampage for which the Tans were renowned, as well as retaliatory attacks by the IRA:

> Police turned up with armoured cars from the jail [Ballymullen Barracks], which was County H.Q. and the other barracks where the present Garda Barracks is. They made four runs through the town and on each run picked up [rescued] a Tan and took them to the barracks at Day Place. The run was out Ballyard, across to Skehanagh, and back into the jail.[35] This would be roughly three miles. The scrap finished up about 2.30.

Mulvihill was ordered to travel to Tralee to investigate 'and to try to prevent further trouble'. Along with John Joe Sheehy,[36] a local IRA commander, he met with senior army men at Ballymullen Barracks:

> ... we decided that we would call up the County Inspector and ask him to meet us. He asked us to come to the Barracks at the Jail. When we got there, he was very high-handed about his men being attacked [in the attempt to steal their vehicle]. I said I was sent over by Dublin to get details and to stop, if possible, any further trouble. He admitted that his men were out of hand, and that he might not be able to control them that night. I left it to John Joe then. He said we did not come up to start trouble

> and were trying to avoid another battle. He also told him we had brought in two machine guns, forty rifle men and hand mined the road in two places. He said: 'We will just have to deal with your men if they come out.'

The death of Percy Hannafin seems to have garnered little sympathy from Mulvihill, who was keen to reassure his counterparts in the RIC that it was an aberration. In a note sent to the district inspector in Killarney, Mulvihill noted that Hannafin and Mullaly 'seem to have taken the law into their own hands and they will have to bear the consequences'.[37]

The comments illustrate the dilemma faced by Mulvihill and other liaison officers at this time. Mulvihill had been on the receiving end of the violence and abuse of the Crown forces over the past two years, his home raided, his family terrorised, his comrades forced to flee to rural hideouts and safe houses. Now he was compelled to communicate – even cooperate – with those same military to keep the peace. He was obliged to ensure that his IRA comrades suppressed their desire to seek vengeance and wreak havoc while the new Irish state was in its infancy. It is clear from a report to the chief liaison officer that Mulvihill was increasingly concerned about the upward spiral of violence in Kerry, and in Tralee in particular. A day after Hannafin and Mullaly were shot and wounded, he wrote, 'Things are in a very serious position in Tralee at present ... threats have been used by both sides, and from what I can understand certain tans [Black and Tans] are preparing to do some of our fellows in ... things are getting worse every day.'[38]

Incidents involving his own IRA company were also reported to Mulvihill by Captain Lancaster and others. In November 1921, for example, he was asked to investigate the alleged kidnapping of three railway personnel in Killorglin by Jack Flynn, IRA commander and a neighbour of Mulvihill's. Flynn and his accomplices, it was suggested, were operating as 'S.F. Police' and had accosted the men for 'refusing to pay I.R.A. fines'.[39] It was clear that it was irresistible to the IRA to take potshots at their enemies, as demonstrated by the fact that two RIC constables, John Lenihan and Patrick Foley, were fired at in Killorglin in November 1921: neither was injured. Foley had been one of those who escaped unscathed from the Ballymacandy ambush of June 1921 and he was a long-time target of the local IRA. The local RIC inspector, T. O'Hanrahan, told Mulvihill that 'there is no necessity for either side ... to run up against each other provided that the terms of the Truce are observed in spirit as well as to the letter'.[40]

The shooting of Constable Charles Ednie in Killarney at the beginning of February 1922 was one of the most controversial of the Truce period and because it occurred a short distance from where Mulvihill was based, it drew him into the heart of an immediate on-site investigation. An 11 p.m. curfew had recently been imposed in the town because of rising political tensions. Mulvihill's memoir contains an account of the incident:

> Patrol [of RIC] was in charge of Nelius McCarthy, Lieutenant in Company (ex-British army man). On the following night, the patrol was in College Street when

> they heard shouting along Main Street, and [a] bunch turned into Henn Street, still shouting.[41] They were called on to halt, and some one of them must have had a revolver and fired a shot. The patrol fired back, and some of them ran back to Main Street, and four threw themselves on the ground. They were ordered to stand up and only three did so. The other man was unconscious and died shortly after.[42] We heard the shooting and got rifles and ran up New Street, Con [O']Leary and myself. As we got to Sewell's Corner, I stumbled over a man lying on the ground. We turned him over and found he was a Tan (drunk). I got two fellows [to] take him to the hotel and guard him there. We contacted the patrol and got their story and as everything was quiet, dispatched it to H.Q. and it was on time for the morning edition of the paper.

The report of the killing of Constable Ednie in the following morning's newspapers provoked a furious response from the military authorities:

> There was hell to pay. Police H.Q., the Division Commissioner, and the Company Inspector found it across the front of the *Irish Independent*.[43] They knew nothing about it. I got a phone call from the County Inspector to know if I and a couple of Brigade Staff would meet him that evening. J.J. Rice, Con [O']Leary, Tom Daly [Dálaigh] and myself went to the Barracks. Earlier that morning

> about 8.30am, Captain Lancaster arrived and asked for me. I went out and he tore at me about the night before. One of his men dead in the Barracks, and another one missing someplace, probably murdered by us etc. I asked him to wait a minute and I went into the hotel and brought out the [drunken] Tan. I told him how we had gone up the street when we heard the shooting and that I fell over him lying drunk on the street. I said we treated him alright. The papers had arrived when he got back to Barracks. When we went to the Barracks later, I had an idea that Lancaster was going to get the works. The County Inspector had heard Lancaster's side of the story. We told him our side. I told him I had sent [a] report to H.Q. and that they had given it to the newspaper ... He at once told Lancaster that he was to blame for the whole thing. He was not actually. It was really an unavoidable accident.

+++

Following the passage of the Treaty by the Dáil and as the British military gradually began to withdraw from the newly established Irish Free State, the position of liaison officer was rendered obsolete. Dan Mulvihill closed his office at the Hibernian Hotel on 7 March 1922.[44] In his final correspondence with the chief liaison officer in Dublin, he noted that: 'The last of the enemy are leaving this County today. Tralee No. 2 barracks was evacuated yesterday, and the C.I. [Chief Inspector] is leaving the place today. This will leave the County clear of Crown Forces.'[45]

Mulvihill's files from his period as liaison officer suggest that he can be credited with playing a key role in keeping the peace in Kerry during the crucial months after the War of Independence ended and the months that followed the signing of the Anglo-Irish Treaty. As the clock ticked inevitably towards Civil War, with the increasingly bitter divisions over the Treaty, Mulvihill ensured that, at a local level, there was no wholesale resumption of warfare between the IRA and the Crown forces. He approached his role with a dry humour and a subtle diplomacy but also a steely determination to keep the peace. He was quick to call out alleged breaches of the Truce by the British forces and the RIC, but he also magnanimously accepted that many on his own side often tested the limits of the Truce – and his patience. Mulvihill noted that 'threats have been made by members of the I.R.A. against certain police – it may be so. I know that the Officers are doing their best to stop that kind of thing as it is a very grave matter. I know that the same applies to certain members of the R.I.C.'[46]

In his memoir, written decades later, Mulvihill noted drily that the end of the Truce period and the evacuation of British troops was 'the end of the rough stuff in Kerry'. Unfortunately for Mulvihill and for Ireland, the 'rough stuff' was far from over. A week after he completed his functions as liaison officer for Kerry, Mulvihill was involved in taking charge of the Great Southern Hotel in Killarney, which had been used by British forces as a base during the War of Independence and the Truce and which was now placed under the control of the Provisional Government. Six months later, however, as Ireland descended into a bitter cycle of fratricide, he would be held in the basement of the same hotel as a prisoner of the new Free State and would be tortured and abused by men he once considered friends and allies.

CHAPTER 8

'The day the split started'

THROUGHOUT HIS LIFE, DAN Mulvihill was always able to pinpoint the precise date on which the possibility of civil war in Ireland became a probability: 'the 9th of April 1922 was the day the split started'. He was referring to the national convention of the IRA, which met in Dublin on that day to continue its deliberations on the controversial Anglo-Irish Treaty and the prevailing political situation.

The signing of the Treaty at the beginning of December 1921 set in train several months of turmoil in Ireland as acrimony grew over the agreement between the British government and the plenipotentiaries of the Dáil. Many of those who had fought for years for the principles declared by the leaders of the Easter Rising were bitterly disappointed – many more were enraged. The much sought-after Irish Republic had not been achieved and for many in the IRA, those who signed the accord were traitors to the cause.

Dan Mulvihill was never in any doubt about his position on

the Treaty and though his own memoir does not specifically record his reaction, he was no doubt influenced by the head of his IRA division, Liam Lynch, with whom he had become increasingly aligned. Lynch was implacably hostile to the agreement from the outset and at a divisional meeting held in December, days after the Treaty was signed by the plenipotentiaries in London, he urged that it be rejected by the Dáil.[1] It is reasonable to assume that Mulvihill was present, because at the end of 1921 he was transferred to the staff of 1st Southern Division as divisional police officer and was formally appointed as aide-de-camp to General Lynch.[2] Locally, Mulvihill and the men of his IRA company were, without exception, vehemently opposed to the Treaty's terms. 'In the Split,' Tom O'Connor of Milltown IRA recalled, 'the active men in the Tan War [in Kerry] remained staunch' to the Republic and opposed the Treaty.[3]

Mulvihill and his comrades were not alone: it is estimated that about three-quarters of the IRA rank and file across the country were opposed to the Treaty. In Kerry, the three brigades were predominantly anti-Treaty, as was the vast majority of the members of Cumann na mBan in the county, including Katie Mulvihill. But there were pockets of support for the Treaty and for the new Irish Free State, with many leaving the IRA to join the new National Army. There were significant divisions within many IRA companies and battalions, which were indicative of the wider split: 'About half of the 3rd Battalion of Kerry No. 1 Brigade in the north Kerry area joined the Free State Army. The IRA in the Listowel district was 45 per cent pro-Treaty, 40 per cent anti-Treaty and the rest "neutral" ... some of the IRA members in Killorglin and Glencar "went Free State" and supported the accord.'[4]

As well as serving on Liam Lynch's staff at this time, Mulvihill was also aide-de-camp to Liam Deasy, who became deputy chief of staff 'when Moss Twomey went with Lynch to G.H.Q.' Lynch, Deasy and Twomey – three of the most influential figures in the IRA in the spring of 1922 – began to play increasingly important roles in Mulvihill's life. Deasy, a native of Bandon, County Cork, was an adjutant with the Cork No. 3 Brigade during the War of Independence, lost his younger brother, Pat, at the Kilmichael ambush in 1920, and fought with Tom Barry at the Crossbarry ambush in 1921. Deasy was a vehement opponent of the Treaty and would go on to be one of the most active anti-Treaty IRA commanders during the Civil War. Maurice 'Moss' Twomey from Fermoy, County Cork, was an adjutant with the Cork No. 1 Brigade and a close ally of Lynch in the 1st Southern Division. He also opposed the Treaty and would later serve as chief of staff of the IRA.

In March 1922 Mulvihill moved to Mallow in County Cork at the request of Liam Lynch. A few weeks previously, Lynch and the 1st Southern Division had taken charge of the army barracks in Mallow following the departure of the British Army. The Provisional Government initially turned a blind eye to the seizure of vacant barracks by anti-Treaty forces.[5] Lynch, along with Deasy and other senior commanders, established a new headquarters for the division – which was predominantly anti-Treaty – and sought out Dan Mulvihill to be based there.

At these headquarters, Mulvihill oversaw the local IRP, which included some recruits from the RIC who had left the force to join the IRA:

> I went to Mallow around 20th March [1922]. I was junior there and was put in charge of [Irish Republican] police: there were ten brigades, sixty battalions, six companies to each battalion, a sergeant and four policemen to each company. A total of nearly 1,900 men. Some of them had been in the R.I.C.: sergeants and inspectors. They were like any crowd of to-day, an odd one here and there very strict, always making trouble ... I was only in that [the IRP] while [the] staff was building.

What was 'building' too was more division within the IRA. A series of meetings of the IRA leaders from across the country in the spring and summer of 1922 set the organisation – and the country – on an irreversible course. Though there were efforts to unite the IRA and to reach a common approach on the way forward, the pro- and anti-Treaty factions were increasingly polarised. In early March, the Provisional Government banned the scheduled national IRA convention, but defiant anti-Treaty officers convened regardless on 26 March at the Mansion House in Dublin. Representatives from fifty-two of seventy-three IRA brigades across the country were present, including Kerry No. 1 and Kerry No. 2. The delegates restated the IRA's loyalty to the Republic and denied any loyalty to Dáil Éireann and the Provisional Government.[6] This was a clear affront to the government and proved that a significant majority of the IRA opposed the terms of the Treaty and refused to accept the legitimacy of the newly established state and its government. Reconvening on 9 April, the convention elected an Army Executive, which appointed Liam Lynch as chief of staff.

Dan Mulvihill, as a senior figure in the 1st Southern Division and as one of the leaders of the Kerry IRA, was among those invited to the conventions at the Mansion House. The importance of the decisions and divisions of 9 April 1922 for Mulvihill personally was evident in the fact that, all his life, he retained in his possession the formal invitation issued by the IRA's director of organisation to the crunch meeting held on that day. Crudely held together with sticky tape, the document survives in Mulvihill's papers in the UCD Archives and includes his own handwritten list of some of the senior IRA leaders in attendance that day, including Lynch, Séumas Robinson, Seán Moylan, Ernie O'Malley and Florrie O'Donoghue. In his memoir, he recorded some of the others who were there, as well as the key staff appointments across the country:

> The [IRA] Convention covered the 32 counties, there were 78 delegates from [the] 1st Southern Division. They appointed a new Headquarters Staff. Liam Lynch was Chief of Staff, Seamus [*sic*] Robinson Vice O/C, Florrie [O']Donoghue, Adjutant.[7] The others were appointed on H.Q Staff – Sean Moylan and Ernie O'Malley.[8] The Northern Divisions Staff were Joe McKelvey, Peadar O'Donnell, W. Gallagher, and M.J. Donnelly. Western Division had

> Mick Kilroy, Liam Pilkington, T. McGuire and Frank Carty. Dublin was Oscar Traynor, Joe [O']Connor, Andy Cooney and Leo Henderson. Southern was Liam Deasy, Pax Whelan, Tom Hayes, 'Free' [Humphrey] Murphy and Sean Hegarty. There were two more conventions before the Civil War, the last one in June, when Florrie Donoghue stood down and Joe Griffin [Tralee] was appointed in his place.[9]

Also present from Kerry at the conventions were the IRA's most senior representatives in the county. In an iconic photograph of the 9 April assembly, which has been widely published over the years, ten other Kerry men can be seen: Denis Daly, Cahersiveen; Tadhg Brosnan, Castlegregory; Con Casey, Tralee; Con O'Leary, Rathmore; Jerome (Jeremiah) O'Riordan, Cahersiveen; Tom McEllistrim, Ballymacelligott; Tom Dálaigh, Firies; Florrie O'Donoghue, Rathmore (Cork No. 1 Brigade); and Humphrey Murphy, Currow, and John Joe Rice of Kenmare, who are seated together in the front row. The handsome twenty-five-year-old Mulvihill stares at the camera from his position in the fourth row, standing beside a partially obscured Tadhg Brosnan and in front of Tom McEllistrim.

The final IRA convention came on 18 June 1922, two days after a general election. By this point, the 'wait and see' faction – including most of the 1st Southern Division, who had wanted to allow negotiations between the Provisional Government and the IRA to continue – and the 'smaller militant group', led by Rory O'Connor and Liam Mellows, were on an unavoidable collision course.[10] In the former group were men like Lynch, O'Donoghue, Deasy, Humphrey Murphy and Mulvihill. If Mulvihill was politically attuned – as he was all his life – he, like the others in the moderate faction, will have paid close attention to the results of the election, the first since the Treaty was signed and in which pro-Treaty parties secured three-quarters of all votes cast, suggesting strong popular support for the agreement. A motion at the convention on 18 June to resume war with the British – which was put forward by Tom Barry and which some believed would unify the IRA – was narrowly defeated. Mulvihill opposed the motion, believing that if the war against the British resumed, the IRA 'would have been well and truly bombed'. The minority militant faction walked out in protest and withdrew to their headquarters at the Four Courts. With two factions now emerging within the anti-Treaty IRA, the government came under increasing pressure to act. Mulvihill recalled:

> At the last convention in June, all the delegates of 1st Southern voted to accept terms, to avoid Civil War. I think that Cathal Brugha [former Minister for Defence] believed that Mick [Michael] Collins would not allow the attack on the Four Courts ... If we accepted [the proposal to resume the war with Britain], we would have had the thirty-two [counties] within five years. We would have gone into the war with the British, and would have been well and truly bombed, which would have been good for us, as the passing years have made us soft.

Mulvihill's remarks about the benefits of a resumption of war – written with the hindsight of decades gone by – points to the types of personal or internal conflict with which IRA volunteers had to tussle at this time. A return to all-out war with the Crown forces must have tempted Mulvihill and some colleagues, who were leading a reinvigorated and resurgent IRA. However, matters quickly spun out of control. Four days after the IRA convention, the assassination of Sir Henry Wilson at the hands of two IRA volunteers occurred in London. A furious British government demanded that the Provisional Government in Dublin respond accordingly. The tensions were exacerbated by the kidnapping by the anti-Treaty IRA of J.J. 'Ginger' O'Connell, a National Army officer. Early on the morning of 28 June 1922, the Four Courts, where Rory O'Connor and his men had remained in defiance of orders to leave, was shelled by the National Army. The Civil War had begun. Mulvihill, like those who had done all they could to prevent war and unify the IRA, reluctantly lent their support to the militants at the Four Courts and joined the war against the Provisional Government.

+++

'The Civil War started with the shelling of the Four Courts,' Mulvihill wrote. 'The boys occupied the Four Courts and took Ginger O'Connell in [*sic*] prisoner.'[11] Despite his own misgivings about the strategy of those occupying the Four Courts, Mulvihill was furious about what he claimed was their resistance to support from the IRA in other parts of the country, which was offered notwithstanding deep reservations among many in the rank in file about a military engagement with the Provisional Government:

> There is one thing I want to make clear. They [the anti-Treaty forces occupying the Four Courts] were asked if they wanted help. Rory O'Connor said 'NO!' They could deal with the situation themselves. We were in a position to throw 10,000 riflemen around the area. We had at least ten thousand rifles in 1st Southern [Division]. We got in a couple of Mausers in April 1922. We had about fifty Thompsons [machine guns] and at least two dozen Lewis guns.

In Kerry, the war erupted two days later when in Listowel there was fierce fighting between the National Army and the anti-Treaty IRA. The first victim of the war in Kerry was Listowel native Private Edward Sheehy, the first of 185 combatants and civilians who would be killed in the fratricide over the following months.[12] Following their seizure of Listowel from the National Army, many in the anti-Treaty IRA in Kerry went to Limerick to defend the 'mythical defence line' between Limerick and Waterford that bordered what became known as the 'Munster Republic', a bastion of anti-Treatyism.[13] Among them was Thomas O'Connor of Mulvihill's company: he was shot through the lung during fighting in Kilmallock but eventually recovered. In the days after Listowel, there were attempts locally to avert further fighting and fratricide.[14] But those efforts and any hopes of peace were short-lived. As Mulvihill recorded: 'We were in the Civil War whether we liked it or not.'

In the days after the assault on the Four Courts, Mulvihill himself returned to Dublin 'on the 6th or 7th July' with Donal O'Callaghan, then the Sinn Féin lord mayor of Cork, and Seán French, a Cork Sinn Féin activist and later a Fianna Fáil TD.[15] Their main business in the capital city was 'the fixing up of funds for the carrying on of the Civil War', including the handing over of 'a large amount' that had been collected across the Southern Division.[16] Just as the trio arrived in Dublin, one of the major figures in Irish republicanism was killed: Cathal Brugha TD, one of the most vehement opponents of the Treaty, died on 7 July 1922 having been shot in the leg during fighting with National Army forces on Thomas Lane in Dublin two days earlier. Mulvihill was among tens of thousands of mourners who attended the funeral on 10 July at Glasnevin cemetery. Shortly after the burial, he 'arranged for about £20,000 to be transferred' from the 1st Southern Division to 'the remains of the Brigade staff' in Dublin.

The following day, Mulvihill became involved in a clandestine mission: to smuggle the political leader of Irish republicanism out of the capital city. Éamon de Valera, who led anti-Treaty TDs out of the Dáil after it voted to accept the Treaty, remained in Dublin 'to keep political work going' despite the outbreak of violence.[17] His focus was on political continuity from the Second Dáil and, as David McCullagh notes, he wanted to get its fifty-seven republican TDs 'out of Dublin so that they could form a government if requested to do so by the anti-Treaty IRA'.[18] On 11 July 1922 de Valera headed south, with the assistance of Mulvihill, who recounted the dramatic exit from Dublin:

> The Four Courts fell. Cathal Brugha was dead. When they wanted to contact Dublin, I was asked to go and I eventually travelled with Donal O'Callaghan, Lord Mayor of Cork, as an Alderman. We wanted to contact the Dublin Brigade. We knew they might need money. Harry Boland was our first contact: I thought a whole [lot] of Harry from the first day I met him in Cork.[19] He fixed a meeting with the Dublin Brigade – they asked if we could fix it to take Dev [Éamon de Valera] out of Dublin. They said he wouldn't have a chance there as they would shoot him on sight. Donal O'Callaghan went to Beggars Bush the next day.[20] He contacted [Garda Commissioner] Eoin O'Duffy and got a permit for the Lord Mayor and two others to travel through to the South.[21]
>
> About 10pm, Donal went to Doctor Murphy's to pick up [the] passenger [de Valera]. Harry Boland and [my]self waited at the Royal Hibernian [Hotel]. I asked Harry to get a chauffeur's cap, which he did, and put De Valera driving, on the principle that no one ever looks at the Lord Mayor's driver. I've seen it mentioned since that he [Dev] was not able to drive, but he was as good a driver as I ever sat in a car with.
>
> We were held up in Naas ... I think our travelling was phoned ahead, as we ran without [a] stop to Callan

> [County Kilkenny] which was the first town held by our crowd. We stopped there as it was daybreak and went to the hotel for a meal. The lady who owned the place recognised Éamon De Valera as she had worked for him in the [United] States. We continued on to Mitchelstown. I left them [de Valera and O'Callaghan] there and they went on to Limerick. I went to Fermoy. Moss Twomey and Tom [O']Connor were in hospital there.[22]

Just a few weeks into the Civil War, Dan Mulvihill was now deep in the 'Munster Republic'. With the government and its army now in substantial command of much of the north, west and east of the country, the only remaining stronghold for anti-Treaty republicans was a few of Munster's counties, including Cork, Kerry, Limerick and Waterford, as well as south Tipperary, the area to the south-west of a line between Limerick city and Waterford city. Liam Lynch, his biographer notes, considered the area, part of his 1st Southern Division, to be 'essential in the formation of a significant block of territory that would be fully occupied by the republican military resistance'.[23] As Mulvihill would quickly discover, however, defending the 'Munster Republic' with dwindling military capacity and against the superior firepower of the new National Army would become increasingly challenging.

Mulvihill's arrival in Fermoy towards the end of July 1922 coincided with a major assault over the following weeks by the National Army on Counties Cork and Kerry. A series of seaborne landings of troops along the coast in early August brought many of the larger towns in both counties under the control of the government. Some 950 troops arrived in Kerry – at Fenit and Tarbert on 2 and 3 August – while hundreds of soldiers led the capture of Cork city from republicans the following week. The capture of Cork was led by Major General Emmet Dalton, Mulvihill's former boss as liaison officer for Kerry and now one of the most effective and trusted officers in the National Army. Mulvihill was in Fermoy as Cork fell, and de Valera arrived there from Mitchelstown just as it was decided to set fire to the local barracks. As anti-Treaty garrisons were forced to withdraw from large towns, the destruction of barracks and similar buildings was common: the aim was to ensure that the building would be rendered useless to the advancing government troops. Dalton's biographer, Sean Boyne, records that as Fermoy Barracks was ablaze, Dan Mulvihill, with the typical black humour for which he was well-known, began to sing 'Home to Our Mountains', a popular aria from the Verdi opera *Il Trovatore*.[24] The song was 'a suitable choice, given that the mountains is where many of the Republicans were heading, to resume guerilla warfare'.[25]

But Mulvihill was still a few weeks away from returning to the mountains of Kerry. In the days after the burning of Fermoy Barracks, Liam Lynch appointed him as command adjutant of the Kerry Command of the Southern Division.[26] As the National Army continued to advance on key towns across Cork, Kerry and Limerick, anti-Treaty republicans were forced into rural areas. Instead of defending towns, militarily, many IRA companies simply abandoned them before withdrawing to the countryside to engage the enemy in the type of guerrilla warfare which had typified the War of Independence.[27] Mulvihill moved north-westwards from Fermoy to Buttevant in north County Cork, before being forced back to Mallow with other anti-Treaty forces:

> I then went on to Buttevant, where we had Division H.Q. Con [O']Leary was in charge of all the Forces in the South, and like Robert E. Lee, he won every battle and lost every victory. We had about 800 men in Buttevant that we had taken prisoner [but] we just had to open the gates and let them out. Buttevant was evacuated and burned at the start of August [1922]. We fell back onto Mallow. The fighting on the Limerick front was abandoned. The Staters [National Army] landed in Cork.[28] Mallow Bridge was blown up and we started to leave.[29] I was last as I stayed to take the messages off the sounder in the station.[30] Divisional Staff took to the country. We were down to Liam Deasy, Tom Daly [Dálaigh], and Ned Murphy and myself in Divisional Staff. We had also Éamon de Valera and Erskine Childers, two of the greats of all time.[31]

The anti-Treaty IRA was reorganised into three different command areas, as Mulvihill detailed:

> The 1st Southern Division was broken up into three Commands: Cork 1 and 2 and Waterford; Cork 3, 4 and 5 and West Limerick; and the three Kerry Brigades. Liam

Deasy, George Power and Pax Whelan, No. 1. Tom Hales, Gibbs Ross, Paddy O'Brien, Sean Moylan and Garrett McAuliffe, No. 2. Con [O']Leary, myself, 'Free' Murphy, J.J. Rice and Jeremiah Reardon, No 3. On the 1st Southern [Division] Staff, Liam Lynch as O/C was a gentle, unassuming type. Liam Deasy was Vice O/C. His book tells the story better than I can.[32] Florrie O'Donoghue was Adjutant: his book tells his story.[33] Joe O'Connor, Quartermaster, was very quiet, a gentleman.[34] Most of the rest of us were half crazy, we could not stop playing tricks on each other. As far as I know there was not a hard drinker in the lot. Moss Twomey was A.D.C. [aide-de-camp] to Lynch. Sean Hyde, a Colonel on H.Q., was seconded to 1st Southern as O/C Cavalry (in Ballincollig).[35] Dr. Connie Lucey was Division MO [medical officer].[36] They were two of the great Cork hurlers. Sean Culhane was Liaison Officer, Cork No. 1. He was in the shooting of Smyth in [the] club in Cork.[37] Also in the shooting of Swanzy in Lisburn (1. Police).[38]

Con Moylan was O/C of Transport, Frank Buckley O/C Supplies, Bill Mahony O/C Signals, Tom Daly [Dálaigh] Asst. Adjt. and 'Free' Murphy Asst. Q.M. [Quartermaster], Phil O'Donnell was Asst. Transport, Moss Walsh, Asst. Adjt., Phil Singleton, Asst. to Noel Murphy, Sean Tuomey Asst. Supplies, and Denny Motherway was Barracks O/C. We had two very famous dispatch riders – Jackie Bolster and Dick Willis, the two inside men in the capture of Mallow Barracks.[39]

> We were the first crowd outside of Dublin in uniform and we seldom wore it outside of Barracks. Except when going out to the Hunt or Point to Point Meetings. We had to do this in our turns. The British had done it before us. Sean Hyde was the only one of us born into this thing. We would go most evenings into the Sports Field which was close to the [Mallow] Barracks and spend an hour or two hurling. One officer was Orderly Officer, Saturday to Monday (in turns). The rest took cars or motor bikes. We had plenty of transport left behind by the British. We had some great weekends. Dr. Connie Lucey, Dr. Paddy Kiely, Sean Hyde, Con Leary, sometimes a few others, went to different places each weekend and held a Dáil Meeting of our own.

As National Army troops continued to push their way into the 'Munster Republic' during August 1922, Mulvihill was on the move once more: 'We billeted in most of the "Big Houses" west and northwest of Mallow, the names I have forgotten. Some were hostile, some not. Two of them I can remember – Coakleys of Mourne Abbey and Callaghans. Late in August the whole crowd assembled in Ballyvourney and that was the final breaking up.'

Towards the end of August, arguably the most pivotal moment of the Irish Civil War occurred about twenty miles from Mulvihill's temporary base in Ballyvourney. On 22 August 1922, as he toured his native County Cork, the chairman of the Provisional Government, General Michael Collins, was killed during an IRA ambush at Béal na Bláth. Writing about the incident many years later, Mulvihill was unsentimental about the loss of one of the most famous Irish political leaders:

> Michael Collins went to London [to negotiate the Treaty] and he was the strong man. He had one weakness – given a few drinks if somebody dared him to do something, said he was afraid, he'd do it. I think that was how Lloyd George got him. Lloyd George never trusted him as he knew that at heart Collins was rabid Irish. Long after the Truce, Collins sanctioned the execution of [Henry] Wilson, for which [O']Sullivan and Dunne were executed.[40] Here was Mick Collins in the middle of a Civil War, coming to his home area and about to make an attempt to stop it so that the whole crowd could get together again. That was [the] time to get rid of him.

Whatever Mulvihill's reaction to the death of Michael Collins, he never forgot where he was when he heard about the ambush that would be such a transformative moment in Irish history. That is because Dan Mulvihill was spending his first night in prison under the custody of Collins' army as a result of his ongoing involvement in the fight against the new Free State.

CHAPTER 9

'Lamb to the slaughter'

BY THE TIME DAN Mulvihill returned to his native county at the end of August 1922, the Civil War had taken a firm grip in Kerry. Many of Mulvihill's comrades who had been fighting in Counties Cork and Limerick retreated to Kerry to take the fight to the National Army, which continued to make progress south-westwards. The early military success of the army in capturing most of the large towns and villages across County Kerry within the early weeks of the Civil War was counterbalanced by the dominance of the anti-Treaty IRA in rural and isolated areas. Guerrilla warfare ensued. The National Army, Gavin Foster suggests, may have secured the larger urban centres in the county, but the situation in rural areas was more complicated:

> Although south-west Kerry – the Third Brigade area – was also considered staunchly republican territory it saw relatively low IRA activity once Free State forces landed in Cahersiveen and took over vacated British garrisons.

> Mid- and north Kerry had more varied experiences and political geographies. Tralee became a major Free State garrison, yet the local population was considered heavily republican whereas Listowel had many strong farmers and shopkeepers who supported the Treaty … yet republican columns operated in the area throughout the Civil War.[1]

Returning to his home at Brackhill near Castlemaine was not an option for Mulvihill. Because it remained a hive of republican activity in the early months of the war, the house was closely watched by the newly established National Army garrison in Killorglin, and arrest, or worse, would have been inevitable for such a senior anti-Treaty IRA leader. His sister Katie's account of this period – provided in her military pension application many years later – offers a glimpse not only of her activities during the early months of the Civil War but also of the dangers of being in the family home at this time:

> From advance of Free State troops to Killorglin [mid-August 1922], house became a centre of activities, again [a] central depot for dispatches. Every day from August on, a number of men had to be fed and a few of them usually stopped [stayed] in house. I was always in possession of a good amount of ammunition left by different men to be held for them. I was under fire on two occasions while trying to get dispatches to Daly's Knockane, nearly all the members of J.E. [Jack] Flynn's Column stopped in house

> at some time during this period. Nursed Jimmy Foley, sick on run, also Ned Langford, U.S.A.[2]

So busy was the Mulvihill home at this time that Katie 'did not know' many of the men who stayed there and were on the run.[3]

Dan Mulvihill was in east Kerry in the second to last week of August 1922 and spent a few nights at the home of the Fleming family at Milleen in Kilcummin, about eight miles from Killarney. The Fleming homestead was, like the Mulvihills at Brackhill, a local headquarters for the anti-Treaty IRA. William Patrick Fleming was a key member of the local IRA and his sister, Marguerite, was O/C of the local Cumann na mBan.[4] From Kilcummin, a large IRA contingent including Mulvihill plotted to attack the National Army base at Hartnett's Hotel in Castleisland. Mulvihill recalled:

> [We went] to Castleisland ... to attack the Free State post there. We took in about fifty [IRA] men. Johnny Connor was across the road in a house with a Lewis Gun.[5] I had taken a mine to the door of the barracks and trailed the wires along the street, when 'Free' [Humphrey] Murphy called it off. Free State troops were supposed to have arrived at bottom of town. I went back and removed the mine and we returned to Kilcummin [to Flemings] where we had stayed the night before.

Mulvihill stayed at Flemings with Con O'Leary, one of his closest friends and allies. O'Leary, a teacher from Rathmore, was quartermaster of his battalion during the War of Independence and second in command to John Joe Rice in the Kerry No. 2 Brigade from October 1921.[6] He was, Mulvihill recalled, 'the best soldier I ever knew'.[7] On the evening of 21 August 1922 Tom Dálaigh arrived 'from G.H.Q. with dispatches', and he asked Mulvihill and O'Leary, who were about to leave, 'to come back to Flemings for the night'. Mulvihill, Dálaigh and O'Leary were all key strategists in the 1st Southern Division and they decided to discuss tactics overnight. It was a costly decision. Acting on a tip-off, at about 6 a.m. the following morning, 22 August, a large contingent of National Army soldiers, under Paddy O'Daly of the Dublin Guard, surrounded the Fleming home at Milleen:

> A local battalion training officer who had stayed neutral went to Killarney and gave us away and Paddy [O']Daly and fifty Dublin Guards came out and surrounded the house.[8] They called on us to surrender and we refused: they opened fire and we fought back. I'd say this lasted about twenty minutes, then they rushed the house and we dropped a Mills bomb [grenade] on them. They stopped and again asked us to surrender, and Margaret [Marguerite] Fleming appeared out of the next room covered with blood. She had two kids there with her, and she put them standing on a bed and stood in front of them. We had meant to fight it out. We just checked it, expecting to be shot as we knew their fellows [were] skilled.

Mulvihill and his comrades surrendered to ensure that medical attention could be sought for Ellie O'Sullivan, a servant girl who was in the house and had fainted. With Tom Dálaigh, Con O'Leary and Will Patrick Fleming, Mulvihill was bundled into the back of an army lorry, placed under arrest and driven to Killarney. They were harassed and abused as they were taken the short distance to jail:

> On the road [to Killarney] we ran into an ambush by our own [IRA] fellows. Every time they [the army] rested on the road, a soldier with a machine gun asked Paddy O'Daly to put us against the fence, that he had one pan of ammo left. His pal had been killed. They told us what they would do to us when they got the chance.

The detainees were held in improvised prison cells at the Great Southern Hotel in Killarney, which was the National Army headquarters in the town. Several rooms in the basement of the hotel had been commandeered by the army to hold prisoners. Conditions in the cells were dreadful: food was scarce, illness was rife, 'the walls were moist and the blankets, the only thing in the cell, were soaking'.[9] The place would soon develop a reputation for the torture and abuse of IRA prisoners as the Civil War intensified. A young man whose brother was an IRA captain was taken there and 'mercilessly beaten to get him to reveal information'. He was then 'thrown down a coal chute and left as dead'.[10] Though Mulvihill does not detail any specific incidents of violence involving himself in his memoir – he was moved from Killarney after a short time – he did offer a vivid portrayal of the way in which many prisoners were treated in the bowels of the Great Southern Hotel in 1922 and 1923:

> Killarney, under the Dublin Guards, was probably one of the most dangerous places in Ireland. Things that are being done in the North at present [early 1980s] were practiced there. Example: knock a fellow across a table, get four fellows to hold hands and legs, another held nostrils until he had to open his mouth to breathe. Officer was waiting and shoved a packet of red paper down his throat. I saw this done to Florrie Donoghue from Glenflesk.[11] I met him later on and asked him what he thought of it. He said 'Christ, Dan, the Black and Tans were only a rumour.'

+++

Mulvihill was only a few days into his prison term when a notorious killing occurred just outside the Great Southern Hotel. On 27 September, a seventeen-year-old member of Fianna Éireann from Castleisland, Bartholomew 'Bertie' Murphy, who had been arrested weeks earlier, was used as a hostage by a National Army convoy that passed through Brennan's Glen near Killarney. Two National Army soldiers, John Martin and Daniel Hannon, had been killed during an IRA ambush. The army's blood was up and the senior officers in the

Killarney Barracks were intent on revenge. Bertie Murphy was on the receiving end of the retaliation, as Mulvihill recalled:

> A convoy [of the National Army] had been to Castleisland and when they were returning, they were asked to take Bertie to Killarney as they had no place to keep him there. They were ambushed on the way back and one of the nicest fellows in the Barracks – ex Irish Guards Sergeant – was killed.[12] The convoy arrived with the dead man and the prisoner [Murphy]. It was his hard luck that a certain officer was present and came on the steps and heard the story, asked a member of the convoy for his rifle and shot Bertie on the steps.[13]

That 'certain officer' was David Neligan, a notoriously ruthless and violent soldier who was synonymous with some of the most brutal episodes of the Civil War in Kerry. Neligan – better known as Michael Collins' 'Spy in the Castle' during the War of Independence – joined the National Army at the beginning of the Civil War. Mulvihill and his fellow prisoners 'knew about the death of Bertie Murphy within a half an hour'. Con O'Leary, who had been arrested with Mulvihill at Kilcummin, was brought from his cell to identify the dead man, but so extensive were Murphy's facial injuries that O'Leary was unable to identify the remains.[14]

Mulvihill and his other cellmates might well have suffered the same fate as Bertie Murphy but for the intervention of Neligan's fellow officer, Paddy O'Daly. O'Daly – a former member of Michael Collins' 'Squad' in Dublin during the War of Independence – has been universally castigated as one of the most brutal and callous leaders of the army in Kerry at this time (with justification), but even he was perturbed by Neligan's propensity for extra-judicial killing. According to an account from prisoner Tom Dálaigh's sister May, it was her brother that Neligan had intended to murder in reprisal for the deaths at Brennan's Glen.[15] In a rare display of concern for republicans who were detained at the Great Southern Hotel, O'Daly is said to have sat outside the cell of prisoners including Tom Dálaigh and Dan Mulvihill, warning that he would shoot any soldier who came near them. O'Daly's actions may have had more to do with the fact that he knew Tom Dálaigh from their shared membership of the IRB in Dublin than any humanitarian concern for his prisoners,[16] but his actions likely spared further killing in the cells of the Great Southern Hotel. Mulvihill recorded that the prisoners remained terrified of Neligan in the aftermath of Bertie Murphy's death:

> The following morning, we noticed sentries doubled at each end of corridor. They told us that he [Neligan] had rushed the corridor the night before and the sentry, an ex-British Army man refused to let him pass. Paddy [O']Daly was in Barracks and was called and he ordered the sentries doubled. We slept in different corners of the room for seven weeks, thinking that if he [Neligan] got through, some one of us would have a chance of getting him. However, he never came.

A few weeks after the death of Bertie Murphy, Neligan and his soldiers went on the rampage in Mulvihill's home village of Milltown.[17] A local publican and bakery owner, Michael Larkin, had been forced to purchase flour stolen by an IRA gang under the command of Mulvihill's close friend and ally Jack Flynn. The army was tipped off and Neligan and his men arrived at Larkin's to accuse the owners of handling stolen goods. As Mulvihill noted, 'they were all drunk and ran amok. They spilled all Larkins' stout and brought him back with them a prisoner.' The following day, as Neligan's men transported the flour to Killarney, a local civilian, Jeremiah Hanifin, was indiscriminately killed when shots were fired by the passing National Army convoy. Hanifin was one of dozens of innocent civilians who lost their lives in the Civil War in Kerry.[18]

Mulvihill and many of the other prisoners in Killarney were moved to Ballymullen Barracks in Tralee in October 1922. Ballymullen was a sprawling former British Army base on the eastern side of Tralee, which had been swiftly captured by the National Army following the landing of troops at Fenit in August. It was during this time that some of Mulvihill's closest friends and allies were executed under the controversial programme of state-sanctioned killings introduced by the Free State government in an attempt to bring anti-Treaty 'Irregulars' to heel: 'I was still in Tralee when Rory, Liam, Dick and Joe were executed. I knew the four of them. Dick Barrett was a special friend.'

Rory, Liam, Dick and Joe were Rory O'Connor, Liam Mellows, Richard (Dick) Barrett and Joseph (Joe) McKelvey, who were among the IRA leaders who survived the National Army assault on the Four Courts at the beginning of the Civil War. Barrett, from County Cork, had been among those who attended the IRA conventions with Mulvihill in Dublin at the beginning of 1922. The four men were controversially executed on 8 December 1922 in reprisal for an attack on two members of Dáil Éireann by the anti-Treaty IRA. The previous day, Seán Hales TD had been shot dead and another Dáil deputy, Pádraic Ó Máille, had been injured in an IRA attack following orders by Chief of Staff Liam Lynch to execute TDs and senators who had voted for controversial public safety legislation, which established military courts with the power to impose the death penalty on insurgents. The four IRA leaders were put to death without trial on the orders of the Minister for Home Affairs, Kevin O'Higgins.[19]

The policy of executions extended to Tralee too, and in January 1923 four Kerry prisoners were killed by a firing squad at Ballymullen Barracks in Tralee on the orders of Paddy O'Daly, recently promoted to the most senior rank in the Kerry Command of the National Army. Whereas O'Daly's predecessor, W.R. English-Murphy, had often resisted the carrying out of executions, the much more ruthless O'Daly 'had no such qualms'.[20] Four prisoners – James Daly from Killarney, John Clifford from Cahersiveen, James Hanlon of Causeway and Michael Brosnan from Ballymacelligott – had been sentenced to death and O'Daly decided to lay down a marker and ensure his reputation for ruthlessness by having the sentences carried out on 20 January. The prisoners were hand-picked for the firing squad by O'Daly as they came from four different parts of the county: this, O'Daly concluded, would send a message to the 'Irregulars' in all parts of the county. The executed men were all known to Mulvihill, particularly James Daly of Knockeenduff, Killarney, who was a long-time member of the Kerry No. 2 Brigade. Mulvihill was with him the night before he went to his death: 'One night I was in the cell talking with Jimmy Daly until about 1 a.m., then went back to my cell. I was awakened by the sound of firing. Jimmy was dead. It could have been me.'

+++

Given the events of the spring of 1923 in Kerry – in which seventeen republican prisoners would be summarily executed in a series of mine explosions by the National Army – it was perhaps fortunate for Dan Mulvihill that he was moved to a prison outside of the county at the end of January:

> After their executions, the Government started to clear C Wing in Mountjoy. They gradually shifted all the senior officers they had arrested to there to be held for execution if any more TDs were shot. Dan Browne,[21] Con [O']Leary, and self were taken from Kerry sometime in January. There was no room for us [in Mountjoy] when we arrived, and we were put in the basement. The Dublin crowd used to say the basement was a place or state of punishment where some poor souls suffered for a time before they went to Glasnevin [cemetery].

According to Mulvihill, there was only one other Kerry prisoner in C Wing of Mountjoy at this time. This was Thomas McElligott – who used the penname 'Pro Patria' – a native of Duagh in north Kerry and a former RIC officer who was the first chairman of the Irish branch of the National Union of Police and Prison Officers. Though not an IRA member, he was jailed twice during the Civil War. Mulvihill and the others 'were there a few days before the Deputy Governor, Paddy O'Keeffe, visited'. Paddy ('Paudeen') O'Keeffe was a familiar face from the past. A native of Nohovaldaly near Rathmore on the Cork–Kerry border, he took part in the 1916 Rising and was a close ally of Michael Collins during the War of Independence. A pro-Treaty TD for Cork, he lost his seat in the June 1922 election and became an officer in the National Army. He was appointed deputy governor of Mountjoy Prison under Governor Phil Cosgrave, a brother of the President of the Executive Council, W.T. Cosgrave. He was a popular if temperamental prison officer. A biographer of O'Keeffe identified the liberal approach to prisoners for which he became known:

> O'Keeffe's regime at Mountjoy was legendary. Surrounded by front-ranking former comrades as prisoners, including the formidable female leaders Maud Gonne MacBride and Mary MacSwiney, he achieved rudimentary control (if not discipline) with least necessary force. His west Cork humour, loaded with irony and expletives, sustained a regime that might easily have collapsed without his basic sense of fairness.[22]

If Mulvihill's memories of this period in jail are anything to go by, O'Keeffe was often kind to the inmates in Mountjoy, if prone to vicious tempers at times:

> He [O'Keeffe] knew us all and saluted us by name. Con [O']Leary who was a friend and neighbour of his asked him why we were being held in the basement. He said: 'I'll tell you then, Con Leary, they [the IRA] burned the President's house, they burned my house, they murdered Sean McGarry's child, and, Con Leary, there's no grain of sugar in Rathmore for the past three months.'[23] They being both from Rathmore, that was the cardinal crime.
>
> 'Paudeen' was about five foot six, with a slight stoop and a big black moustache. He was always in uniform, and a gun strapped to his thigh. To every fellow inside [in prison] who had been going to films, he was a figure straight out of the *Keystone Cops*. I had been an ardent film fan, going to two pictures each night when I had the funds. I don't think any of the fellows disliked him but every time they saw him, he reminded them of something they used to shout at in the pictures.

On one occasion, when the prisoners mocked and abused O'Keeffe in the presence of a visiting priest who was administering ashes on Ash Wednesday, the deputy governor reacted furiously:

> That night after lights out the Oriel House [detectives] crowd arrived, most of them drunk, and each had a revolver.[24] They started inside the gate at the first cell and got everything in the cell out on the ground floor. They then locked the doors as they went. Any fellow who was in bed was left in his undergarments. We were on the first landing and saw what was going on, and we put what we had on us. It was not much. I think it was Ben Brady of Donegal, who was in the cell with me, and when they arrived we threw everything in the cell over the rails to the ground floor and were locked in. They finished the Wing about twelve o'clock. After they left, the heating was turned off, and we were left locked up until Friday morning. It was freezing at the time and all I can remember of it was walking up and down the cell for an hour trying to get warm, lying on the floor until cold, then sitting up.

For the several months they spent in C Wing of Mountjoy, Mulvihill and the other Kerry men found themselves in some prestigious company:

> We were shifted to C Wing the following day. C Wing held all the senior [IRA] officers of the thirty-two counties who had been captured up to that time. I will give the names of the ones I knew and remember. Count Plunkett, first T.D. to have been elected, lost sons in the Rising.[25] Dr. [James] Ryan,[26] Paddy Rutledge,[27] Eamon Donnelly,[28]

> Sean Russell,[29] Brian O'Higgins,[30] Peadar O'Donnell,[31] Ben Brady,[32] Peadar Duignan,[33] Andy Cooney.[34] I could give a lot more but I might make mistakes. The four of us [Mulvihill, Tom Daly, Will Fleming and Con O'Leary] were the late arrivals.
>
> Everything went on there. It was a huge university. We had Irish, English, French, Maths, Engineering, Civics and Newspaper. We also ran a Debating Society. This and Irish were my two favourites. I had no Irish when I went there first, and I haven't enough to get by with now. Through the debating I got very friendly with Seán Russell.
>
> I slipped one day in the ring and hurt my back and was in bed for some weeks. It has never left me since. I had been a good footballer, hurler, jumper, runner and 120 yards hurdler, also the discus, but never again ... looking back now, I realise, we were nearly stone mad! We were all tricking on each other and we were always in trouble with the prison staff.

Though Mulvihill's memoir does not detail what day-to-day life was like in Mountjoy, his comrade Tom Dálaigh provided an account of the miserable daily dining regime in the prison during their months of incarceration:

> Breakfast: a mug of porridge oatmeal and Indian meal mixed, a loaf of bread which cannot be eaten until toasted, a sample of butter and a mug of alleged tea and

> half a mug of milk. Dinner: ½ loaf of bread, mug of soup (hot water with suggestion of meat) 2 or 3 potatoes and a piece of meat, like rubber with uneatable cabbage. Supper: same as breakfast but without the oatmeal. Very often butter has to be refused by the M.O. [medical officer], it being rotten.[35]

+++

While Mulvihill remained in jail through the spring and summer of 1923, the Civil War reached its violent zenith in his native county. Almost forty combatants died during the so-called 'Terror Month' of March 1923 in Kerry. The deaths of five National Army soldiers in an IRA booby-trap mine in Knocknagoshel at the beginning of March triggered a series of vicious reprisals in which seventeen IRA prisoners were summarily executed by the army using explosives as prisoners cleared roads of obstructions at Ballyseedy, Bahaghs and Countess Bridge.[36] Mulvihill would remain a close friend of the sole survivor of the massacre at Ballyseedy, Stephen Fuller (a distant cousin), and was later best man at his second wedding.[37] Fuller managed to evade death at Ballyseedy but remained physically and psychologically scarred for the rest of his days. Meanwhile, in April, three IRA volunteers and two soldiers died following a siege at Clashmealcon Caves in north Kerry, and a further three IRA members were executed at Tralee jail for their roles in that episode.[38] The death of Mulvihill's friend and hero, Liam Lynch, on 10 April, heralded the end of the war, which finally came at the end of that month. It was a conflict that had claimed 185 lives in Kerry alone, an average of one casualty per day.[39]

The end of the Civil War did not mean freedom for Dan Mulvihill and the estimated 12,000 republican men and women who were still in prison. Despite the cessation in hostilities and the anti-Treaty order to dump arms, the Free State government was fearful that a mass release of internees could reignite the conflict and allow the anti-Treaty IRA to regroup and mobilise once more. Accordingly, prisoners who had been jailed over the preceding months continued to be detained. In May 1923, as the Civil War petered out, Mulvihill was on the move again, this time to the Curragh Camp in County Kildare, which was dubbed 'Tintown' by its internees and which had been handed over to the National Army by the British Army after the War of Independence. A series of former army huts were used to house a growing number of prisoners:

> We were shifted to Tin Town 3 sometime in May. I'd say there were about 4,000 in the Camp. Football was being played there all day. We played inter-provincial matches. Leinster always won. They had about 3,000 from Leinster, and we had only 300 from Munster. My injured back and the fact that I had been inside one year put me out of it. I played alright when my back was well and could outfield anyone but could not hold the hour. When my back was right, I could outrun or outjump anyone in the camp.

> Joe Stynes was the outstanding footballer in Camp.[40] Paddy Clifford, Ballymac and Armitage of Tipperary were next. Tin Town 3, like all camps was run by camp staff. We did our own cooking. There was always a few [escape] tunnels going on. I was too tall for that. We had a very good escape system working. A P.A. in Camp would take two fellows to the verge of camp and hand them over to an outside contact. This was working perfect, as it was impossible to get a perfect count [of prisoners] ... there were over 1,000 fellows sleeping in double deckers [bunk beds]. It was coming to our turn when the whole thing blew up. Paddy Mullins was recognised near his home in Galway though he was still supposed to be a prisoner. The count was still correct though about eight fellows had got away. They knew it had to be an inside job. The P.A. was an I.R.A. man and used to take letters for us when he went to Dublin with dispatches. He knew the risk, of course. I gave him about a dozen letters one time as he was going to Dublin the following day.

In December 1923 Corporal Joseph Bergin was captured and killed by his army colleagues on suspicion that he was carrying messages to and from Tintown for the IRA prisoners. 'That,' Mulvihill noted, 'ended our hopes of escape.'

The mood among IRA prisoners darkened as the autumn of 1923 approached and they became increasingly frustrated at their continued detention. Even though the Civil War had ended several months previously, the Free State government remained apprehensive about a large release of internees who were openly hostile to the state. Some prisoners who were considered low risk had been freed during the summer, but over 10,000 anti-Treaty men and women remained incarcerated. As frustrations and tensions grew, prisoners in Mountjoy decided to go on hunger strike in protest. The hunger strike began on 13 October and prisoners in camps and jails across the country quickly followed. Within a short time, about 8,000 IRA and Cumann na mBan prisoners were refusing food.

Prisoners at Tintown in Kildare were among them. Dan Mulvihill is included in a list of IRA prisoners on hunger strike in Hut 17 at Tintown 3 in a report in the republican newspaper *Éire* on 10 November.[41] This means that he had been refusing food for at least four weeks by mid-November, by which time over 2,000 prisoners had already withdrawn from the hunger strike. Among those incarcerated, there were significant divisions about the merits of the strike. The strategy met with opposition from some Kerry prisoners, including Billy Mullins from Tralee, who had fought alongside Mulvihill at the Ballymacandy ambush in 1921. Mullins was sceptical:

> In order to have a successful hunger-strike, you must have dedicated and sincere men who are prepared to go a long way ... I fought tooth and nail against such a move, pointing out that it could not possibly succeed ... I pointed out to the [Prisoners'] Council that there would be men running to the cookhouse after two, three and four days ... I was overruled.[42]

Even Austin Stack, arguably Kerry's most high-profile anti-Treaty IRA leader, had doubts, writing: 'It will be terrible should they die like this ...'[43] Mulvihill also struggled to see the long-term political or tactical benefits. In the process, his health suffered considerably:

> Suddenly the big hunger strike was ordered. I don't want to say anything nasty only that it could serve no purpose. I felt like a lamb to the slaughter. I was fourteen stone when it started, I was nine when it ended. I went in with a good stomach, came out with a bad one. The reverse happened to a pal of mine, Paddy Barry, Tralee. His stomach had been giving him trouble, but the long fast on salt and water gave it a chance to heal and he told me afterwards that it was perfect.

During the third week of November, two prisoners – Andy O'Sullivan from Cavan and Denis Barry from Cork – died, and shortly afterwards the remaining prisoners ended the hunger strike, forty-one days after it had begun. The Catholic primate, Cardinal Logue, had called for the release of prisoners and some 2,600 were freed at the end of November. Not so Dan Mulvihill, who spent Christmas 1923 at Tintown: 'The [Tintown] Camp was nearly empty for Christmas, and I was back home early in 1924, a big soft heap with a bad back.'

Though Mulvihill likely suffered the side-effects of the hunger strike in later years, he was spared the worst impacts of going so long without food. The forty-one days without food contributed to the premature death of many of his comrades. Austin Stack – who was not released from jail until August 1924 – died in 1929, having never fully recovered his health. Mulvihill's friend and comrade, Tom Dálaigh of Knockaneacoolteen, died in 1939 at the age of just forty-one, wracked by pulmonary tuberculosis and the after-effects of his hunger strike.

+++

The war in Kerry had taken an enormous toll. As documented elsewhere by this author, combatants and survivors suffered years of medical and psychological problems, the families of those killed and injured on both sides experienced poverty, intimidation and grief, while the wider civilian and business community bore the brunt of the economic stagnation and turmoil for many years.[44] With a few exceptions, Mulvihill does not document his own personal traumas after the years of combat, imprisonment and hunger strike. The physical toll of over forty days without food had left him 'a big soft heap', but neither his IRA pension application nor any medical reports point to the neurasthenia (post-traumatic stress disorder) and other mental health problems that so many of his peers endured. Perhaps he was one of the lucky ones, fortunate to possess an inner resilience, mental fortitude or good physical fitness, which helped him to cope with the effects of the war and depriving himself of food. Or perhaps he endured flashbacks, depression and mental disturbance in private and in silence. Mulvihill's testimony and the clues about his character and attitude to life contained in his memoir suggest he fell into the former category and, because he continued to be involved in republicanism throughout subsequent decades, he may well have avoided the traumas that forced many of his contemporaries to return to civilian life or to succumb to psychological troubles and poor physical health after the end of the Civil War.

Writing about the conflict some sixty years later, Mulvihill was philosophical about the Civil War. He was torn between accepting the horror of what had occurred and regret that the anti-Treatyites had not prevailed. He regretted that his comrades across the whole island had not risen as one:

> I saw the implications of the Civil War. I knew we were bequeathing a task to a future generation ... [I] couldn't [accept] the fact that everything we had fought for had been thrown away. It had a terrible effect on them [anti-Treatyites]. I knew we could have won it [the war] in the first week if the crowd had realised what was happening, but our crowd being beaten [in the Four Courts] meant to me that there would be no chance until Ulster started herself. You cannot free a man who is making no effort to free himself.

CHAPTER 10

'We raided once a month'

WHILE DAN MULVIHILL SPENT the final months of the Civil War in jail, and during his six weeks on hunger strike, his sister Katie continued to offer refuge at Brackhill to IRA men, many of whom remained on the run through the end of 1923 and into 1924. The end of the war did not mean a return to normality (or safety) for anti-Treaty men and women, who continued to be subjected to intimidation and whose homes were frequently monitored and raided by the National Army. 'I know we had two or three staying with us until Christmas 1923 and an odd one until the summer of 1924,' wrote Katie when listing the IRA men whom she had nursed and catered for during the Civil War. Among those she looked after was Tom O'Connor of the Milltown Company, who continued to recuperate after being badly wounded during fighting in Kilmallock in County Limerick.

Close attention continued to be paid to republican homes and activists during the general election campaign of August

1923. The election was the first since the Civil War ended and pitted the governing pro-Treaty party, Cumann na nGaedheal, against the anti-Treaty republicans.[1] IRA and Cumann na mBan members played a leading role in the election campaigns of anti-Treaty candidates in Kerry and beyond. There were several episodes of violence during the election and the President of the Executive Council, W.T. Cosgrave, was assaulted and abused during a visit to Tralee. Raids by the National Army on the homes of republicans continued during the campaign and forced many of those who were not still in prison to remain on the run, among them Thomas McEllistrim, who, even though he was a candidate in the 1923 election, had to remain in hiding and could not campaign for votes. The result in Kerry was a huge boost for the republicans, who secured 45 per cent of the votes cast and won four Dáil seats. Cumann na nGaedheal, which won a third of first preferences, secured the remaining three seats. Among those elected on the anti-Treaty side in Kerry was Mulvihill's former IRA comrade Paddy Cahill from Tralee.

If Dan and Katie Mulvihill escaped the immediate psychological problems which so many other combatants endured, they did not escape the clutches of the economic hardships of the months and years after the Civil War. Their eldest brother, Matthew, died in 1924 in an unspecified accident.[2] In the same year, the Mulvihills sold their home and farm at Brackhill and moved to a smaller house and holding a short distance away. The family was 'nearly £2,000 in debt'.[3] Agriculture, the family's main source of income, was depressed in the early 1920s, reflecting the wider economic misery of the time as the new Irish Free State grappled with multiple social and economic challenges. Mulvihill was without a steady income. He 'started playing football again' but his earlier prison injury endured: 'When my back was alright, I played a good match, then it went again. I was called for the trials for the 1924 [Kerry] team but did not go as my back was acting up.'

The anti-Treaty IRA, defeated in the Civil War, was in rag order in the immediate aftermath of the conflict. Despite its strong showing in the election in Kerry, the Sinn Féin party was bedevilled by poor organisation, demoralisation and a lack of resources. Efforts by Mulvihill and others to reorganise and rejuvenate the IRA in mid-Kerry were a failure: 'We made one [IRA] brigade of the county and half a dozen of us tried to run it. We had nothing left in 1925.' Reorganisation and mobilisation were hampered by high levels of unemployment and emigration among anti-Treaty combatants after the Civil War. Many were denied work for political reasons and were dismissed from their jobs.[4] Families of combatants experienced poverty and isolation. For many, emigration to the United States and further afield was the only option. At the beginning of 1925 Mulvihill's comrade Tom Dálaigh reported to IRA headquarters about the plight of anti-Treatyites in Kerry:

> EMIGRATION: ... the number of Volunteers who have emigrated is very large. In compiling the figures, I only took the number of those who had been actually engaged in the recent war. Numerous others intend emigrating ...

> UNEMPLOYMENT: ... a great deal of distress prevails throughout the area ... [in some areas] the position is worse than it has been for many previous years.[5]

With the IRA in disarray and with limited employment prospects, it was perhaps inevitable that Mulvihill would follow the path of so many of his IRA comrades by leaving Ireland. His passport from the time dates his departure from the port of Cobh to New York – on Immigration Visa Number 14235 – to 9 November 1925.[6] However, unlike so many of his peers, his time in America was brief:

> I went to Chicago and got on well there. I got a bad cold in 1926 and went to a doctor [in the United States]. He told me I was rotten with T.B. [tuberculosis]. I was not feeling too bad but decided that if I was going to get sick, Chicago was the last place I'd like to be, so I said I'd go back to Ireland. I had just got a good job in the Forrest [*sic*] Preserve.[7] When I landed back in Cork, I made off [*sic*] a friend of mine, a doctor, and told him the yarn. He examined me and found two spots in my lung and decided on X-ray and sputum tests. Then I got the all clear from him.

Whether Mulvihill remained a member of the IRA throughout the remainder of the 1920s cannot be verified with certainty from his own accounts or from records of the time. But it is likely that there was no break in his involvement in the years after the Civil War. In his own account, he describes, albeit vaguely, how 'we raided once a month up to 1930 and from then on once a week. At that period, friend or foe would make for the ditch if he heard a car coming.' Despite the challenges it faced, the IRA in Kerry in the mid-1920s remained a force, and historian Brian Hanley puts the strength of the Kerry brigades at just under 500 in 1926.[8]

There is no evidence that Mulvihill was ever a member of a political party and, unlike so many anti-Treaty combatants, he does not appear to have joined or taken up any role in Fianna Fáil, the newly formed republican party established by Éamon de Valera in 1926. Fianna Fáil emerged as the leading anti-Treaty voice in Irish politics and many of Mulvihill's peers, including his friend and neighbour Jack Flynn, immersed themselves in the new party. Flynn was elected to Kerry County Council in 1926 and was to have a long career in politics. Though Fianna Fáil abstained from the Dáil initially as a result of the party's refusal to accept the Oath of Allegiance to the Crown, the assassination of the Minister for Justice, Kevin O'Higgins, in 1927 by opportunistic members of the IRA, and new legislation on the Oath of Allegiance, which required candidates to commit to swearing the oath if elected, forced Fianna Fáil's hand, and its TDs entered the Dáil to pursue the parliamentary path. From the perspective of Mulvihill and his colleagues in the IRA, the most significant consequence of the killing of O'Higgins was 'an avalanche of repression', including draconian new public safety legislation, which involved a clampdown on IRA activity by the Cumann na nGaedheal administration.

Despite the drift towards politics by many of his peers, and the perils of remaining involved in paramilitary activity, Mulvihill persisted in his commitment to militant republicanism, and in the 1930s he became ever more radical in his outlook and activities. At the beginning of the decade, he joined a new left-wing splinter group within the IRA, which further highlighted his militant inclinations. Named Saor Éire (Free Ireland), it was difficult to argue with the contention of one American military observer that it was 'frankly communist in outlook'.[9] Mulvihill might not have been a communist, but he was radical in his politics and was attracted to an organisation which had socialist as well as republican policies. Established in September 1931, a police report from the time described Saor Éire as 'quasi-political' and with intentions to 'replace Sinn Féin'.[10] Little is known about the extent of its membership in Kerry. Its first national congress was held in Dublin in September 1931. The new party set its sights somewhat wider than anti-Treaty republicanism. It described itself as 'The Irish Workers' and Farmers' Republican Party'. Apart from breaking 'the connection with England', there was a focus on vesting 'political and economic power within the Republic in the working class and working farmers'.[11] Among its leading members was the Donegal radical and socialist Peadar O'Donnell, with whom Mulvihill had spent time in jail during the Civil War. 'We were all in Saor Éire,' Mulvihill recalled, 'but we would back anyone to get the [Cumann na nGaedheal] Government out.'

The new party was widely condemned by the Catholic Church, which stoked paranoia about communism in Ireland

and the influence of Moscow in Irish politics. Among its staunchest critics was the Bishop of Kerry, Dr Michael O'Brien, who was a brother of Bryan (Bryannie) O'Brien, a close ally of Mulvihill's in the IRA during the War of Independence and the Civil War. Bishop O'Brien angrily dismissed Saor Éire as distributing 'poisonous propaganda', adding that it was 'not a continuation of the IRA' and that 'funds are supplied from Moscow'.[12] In October 1931 the organisation was banned by the government and it disintegrated shortly afterwards. Mulvihill, however, 'kept on with the IRA' and voted for Fianna Fáil at the 1932 general election in which Jack Flynn was elected a TD. Éamon de Valera, whom he had helped to smuggle out of Dublin at the beginning of the Civil War, became president of the Executive Council, and Fianna Fáil replaced Cumann na nGaedheal in government. De Valera immediately suspended public safety legislation and released many IRA prisoners who had been jailed by the Cosgrave government.[13]

However, the close relationship between the IRA and the new Fianna Fáil administration was short-lived, and following a number of killings and episodes of violence, the IRA was declared an illegal organisation by the government in 1936. Mulvihill, like many IRA members, was disillusioned by the failure of Fianna Fáil to declare and achieve the republic which they had fought for: 'The promises we got [from Fianna Fáil] could not be fulfilled as the outgoing crowd [Cumann na nGaedheal] covered their tracks with Acts of Parliament.'

Political tensions were further heightened in the mid-1930s with the rise of the Blueshirts, a paramilitary, uniformed group that used fascist slogans and salutes and clashed repeatedly with the IRA. The Blueshirts – which provided protection for Cumann na nGaedheal members at public meetings – were quite active in Kerry, with over 1,700 members in the county in 1934, and there were several violent clashes with republicans during Blueshirt rallies and social events. The most significant episode was an attempt by the IRA in Tralee to assassinate the Blueshirt leader, Eoin O'Duffy, in October 1933.[14] During a visit to the town, O'Duffy was seriously wounded during a violent melée. Among the plotters was Dan Keating of Castlemaine, with whom Mulvihill had fought in the Ballymacandy ambush.[15] Mulvihill does not record if he was involved in any of these episodes, but he later recounted the political tensions that prevailed during the 1930s, including fears that the Blueshirts would seek to overthrow the Fianna Fáil government in a coup: '[There was] an incident (right after Fianna Fail winning operations [in 1932] were made for takeover). I won't mention who was at back [behind it] but W.T. Cosgrave got wind of it, and he put his foot down and stopped it. After the finish of the Blueshirts, we had a new C.I.D. [Detective Unit].'

By the mid-1930s, the IRA in Kerry remained intact, if not as vibrant or active as it had been in previous years. Though precise data is limited, there were some 190 members in the Cahersiveen area, 120 in Dingle, 300 in Killarney and 140 in Tralee.[16] The principal leaders in Kerry were John Joe Rice of Kenmare and John Joe Sheehy from Tralee. There is nothing to suggest that Mulvihill held a rank of any significance at this time. If he remained a member in the 1930s, it was a period generally of inactivity and decline, despite an enduring network of members: Mulvihill's days of combat and militant republicanism were largely behind him.

+++

As the world drifted towards war in the late 1930s and as British Prime Minister Neville Chamberlain and others sought to appease Adolf Hitler to avoid an international conflagration, the very final physical presence of the British military in the Irish Free State came to an end. Under the terms of the Anglo-Irish Treaty, the British, for reasons of international defence, had been permitted to maintain naval bases at Lough Swilly in County Donegal and Berehaven and Spike Island in County Cork. Following negotiations between the Irish and British governments during the 1930s, and as an economic war between their two countries continued, the British agreed to abandon the so-called Treaty Ports. The handover of Spike Island in Cork Harbour took place, with great fanfare, on 11 July 1938, the anniversary of the Truce that ended the War of Independence. Dan Mulvihill was a special guest at the ceremony at Spike Island at the personal request of Éamon de Valera.[17] *The Times* of London reported on the arrival of de Valera and his delegation:

> Amid the booming of guns the last British troops stationed at Spike Island in Cork Harbour this evening handed over custody of the island and the adjoining

> fortifications to the troops of Eire. For the ceremony of taking over the fortifications the Government of Eire sent out a number of invitations, the guests including Ministers, members of the Dáil and Senate, and leaders of the old Irish Republican Army. A decorated train brought the guests from Dublin to Cobh, and a tender carried them to Spike Island, where about 300 Irish troops had already landed under Major Maher. The British had already departed when Mr. de Valera and Mr. Frank Aiken, the Minister for Defence, arrived in a launch, being greeted by a salute of 19 guns. The troops were formed up around the flagstaff and Mr. de Valera ran up the tricolour national flag of Eire over Westmoreland Fort to the accompaniment of a salute of 21 guns.[18]

An image that was published in the press of the arrival of the Irish government party on a flotilla of boats shows Mulvihill on a smaller boat adjacent to de Valera's, whose party included the Minister for Defence, Frank Aiken, the Minister for Agriculture, Dr James Ryan, and the Minister for Justice, P.J. Ruttledge. The Minister for Defence, according to Mulvihill's obituary, invited him to take part in raising the National Flag during the ceremony.[19] Mulvihill's invitation to Spike Island and his prominent role in the proceedings emphasised not only a recognition of his role in the IRA of the revolutionary years but also his enduring personal loyalty to and friendship with Éamon de Valera. Despite the cordiality and celebration at Spike Island, a dark shadow hung over the occasion as the onward march of Hitler's armies continued across Europe and war loomed. And despite Ireland's neutrality, the country would be greatly impacted by the conflict. As he stood to attention for the national anthem on Spike Island on that summer evening in 1938, Dan Mulvihill would not have known that he would play an important role during the war years and what became known in Ireland as 'The Emergency'.

CHAPTER 11

'Bitterly anti-Irish and anti-Catholic'

DAN MULVIHILL WAS A self-styled radical and maverick throughout his life, but he was also a pragmatist. The outbreak of the Second World War in 1939 forced him to weigh up his options, personally and politically. He played no role in the IRA during the conflict. The organisation was still banned by the government, but many of its senior figures looked upon the war as an opportunity to collaborate with others – including Nazi Germany – to achieve the reunification of Ireland and an Irish republic. An IRA bombing campaign was carried out in England in 1939 and 1940 under the so-called 'Sabotage Plan' and in December 1939 the IRA raided the Magazine Fort in Dublin, stealing a large stock of arms and ammunition. As Eunan O'Halpin states, this highly embarrassing incident 'underlined the internal security menace posed by the IRA, and the organisation's potential as a "fifth column" in the event of an external attack'.[1] Mulvihill appears to have had no appetite for collaboration with Nazi Germany or for being part of this 'fifth column'. He recognised wider political realities and, despite his revulsion for what he considered to be an illegitimate political entity, he knew that the choice was between possible jail time with his former comrades or aligning himself with the Free State, which faced the threat of invasion from the Nazis or the Allies for their own strategic gain: 'At the start of the [Second World] War, I found myself faced with the situation of going into the L.D.F. [Local Defence Force] or going into the Curragh [prison]. I had had enough of the Curragh and ... I decided I'd stay where I could get a rifle.'

The LDF was one part of the Irish government's response to the war. In 1939 Ireland was 'extraordinarily ill-prepared to defend itself', with an ill-equipped and under-resourced army just 6,000 strong and without an air corps or naval defences of any description.[2] This left the country exposed to invasion or violation by any of the belligerents in the looming conflict. On 1 September 1939 the government, led by Fianna Fáil and Éamon de Valera, ordered a mobilisation of all defence forces and began a recruitment campaign to supplement the army. The speed with which Hitler's army pushed through the Low Countries and into France shocked the Irish government. There was a recognition that Ireland was vulnerable to attack on two fronts. Ireland 'was an obvious candidate for invasion: by Germany, to seize ports and airfields with which to assist the invasion of the British mainland and to threaten Britain's Atlantic lifeline; and by Britain, to gain control of the Treaty

Ports and other military bases or to pre-empt or repel a German attack'.[3]

Mulvihill joined the Local Security Force, part of which was reconstituted as the LDF at the beginning of 1941. This reserve force of volunteers acted as an auxiliary or supplementary force to the National Army, which had grown to over 40,000 in number by the spring of 1941. Though poorly organised and poorly equipped, the force was an important buttress to the army. National security and political stability necessitated that many anti-Treaty activists were readily admitted to the Local Security Force, despite concerns that the army might become vulnerable to infiltration by the IRA:

> We built up a very good organisation against what we thought was coming. Peter Browne, who was over the county, was an Ex-Battalion O/C.[4] Donal O'Sullivan, a teacher, found himself facing the Army or the Curragh, he was the Captain. Florrie Lawlor, Lieut., was an I.R.A. man also. We were lucky in the South. From M.J. Costelloe down the line all key jobs were held by I.R.A men. I can't vouch for any other place. We had four leaders of the L.D.F., Tom Connor (based in Tralee), who had been wounded in Civil War, Alfie Smith, Killarney, whose brother was interned in the Curragh, and Ned Mahony, Caherciveen and self in the old battalion ... Liam Deasy, ex Div. O/C who also was an Officer. If England had invaded, it would have been fought to the last ... Tom Mac [McEllistrim] came to me and told me

> that Dev [de Valera] had called him in the evening before and told him to tell us that it could come at any time that he was only playing them off from day to day.

The growing concern about the prospect of attack or invasion, by either Britain or the Germans, highlighted the need for increased intelligence and information. Given his background and experience, Mulvihill was headhunted by an old friend for an important role in a new and clandestine wing of the army reserve. It was set up by his former IRA comrade Florence O'Donoghue. A native of Rathmore on the Cork–Kerry border, O'Donoghue had resigned from the IRA in disgust at the beginning of the Civil War and returned to civilian life.[5] During the 1930s he 'stayed largely aloof from an unsteady political situation in Ireland', but at the outbreak of the Second World War, he joined the National Army, rising to the rank of intelligence officer in the Southern Command.[6] With intelligence proving to be crucial in weeding out any plans by the British or the Germans to invade Ireland, O'Donoghue recognised the experience that many of his old IRA colleagues had in gathering information and decided to put it to good use. He conceived the Supplementary Intelligence Service (SIS), a secret body which was used to monitor civilians who were believed to be sympathetic to the belligerents in the war or involved in any way in supporting potential military incursions in Ireland. So secretive was the SIS that its members never appeared on any army membership lists.

The backbone of the SIS was experienced anti-Treaty

IRA men in Munster, particularly those who 'would not dream of taking a Free State oath or of wearing a Free State uniform' but who were keen to keep a close eye on 'west Brits' in their localities, with official sanction.[7] To his new service, O'Donoghue recruited 'selectively, choosing many former colleagues from the independence struggle'.[8] Among them was his friend and ally Dan Mulvihill:

> Florrie [O']Donoghue came down and told me a story that I found was correct. Something that could be nearly impossible happened in Dublin. A complete list of all British agents in Ireland fell into the hands of Irish I.O.s [intelligence officers]. Within days they were tipped off and the whole lot were switched. Some of them had been well-known and the trouble was to trace the new ones.
>
> We started an Intelligence Service of our own outside of the L.D.F. Florrie was in charge of the Southern Command, I was in charge of Kerry, and in a few months, working on our old methods, we accumulated a pile of information. I had some of the most unlikely people working for me. The best in Kerry was the late Chief Superintendent Harry O'Meara. We confiscated a letter from a L.D.F. officer offering himself and his unit [to the British] in case of an invasion. Harry was in favour of putting a label on him. I put the case to H.Q. They advised against trying him, as we would have to reveal the fact that we were censoring. He had only written to a regular Officer. We just got him out of the ranks.

The area covered by Mulvihill 'started in the Dingle Peninsula, and went through Ballingarraun[9] across to Caragh Lake, to MacGillicuddy's [Reeks], to Tomies Mountain, on to Flesk Castle, to the County Bounds and on to Cork City'. He began to send regular reports to Florence O'Donoghue about those he and others considered to be sympathetic either to the British or the Germans. The correspondence, held in the National Library, points not only to Mulvihill's skills as an intelligence gatherer with his ear to the ground, drawing on information from his old networks in the IRA, but also highlights a growing paranoia about the potential for trouble from Nazi sympathisers, as well as 'anti-Irish' and British residents. A small sample of the 'secret' and 'absolutely confidential' instructions issued to SIS members survive in Mulvihill's private papers and highlight the extent of the monitoring of individuals under suspicion. Even those driving a particular type of car – especially those manufactured in Britain – were not to be trusted: 'Instruct all concerned to keep special watch for the movements of the following cars: ZB 3609, 8 HP FORD, ZB 1385 MORRIS. Observations of those cars in your area should be reported as soon as possible, but the report need not be made by telephone. Contacts made by the occupiers of the cars should also be reported.'[10]

Any 'suspects' who received registered letters were also deemed to be worthy of investigation unless there was some 'legitimate transaction'.[11] Mulvihill not only carried out the orders he received from headquarters, he also took it upon himself to issue instructions to his own network of spies, the names of whom are not contained in his papers (for obvious reasons) but likely comprised former and current IRA volunteers with whom he had worked closely in the past. In a communiqué titled 'Secret: Danger [of] British Landing – Instructions to I.O.s' and dated 9 September 1943, Mulvihill outlined what the SIS would be required to do in the event of an invasion by a foreign power:

> If invasion takes place, our work will to a great extent change over to combat intelligence and in this the intimate local knowledge which will result from a study of each area will be invaluable. It is hoped to issue some notes on Combat Intelligence from time to time, which may be of assistance in this connection. In the meantime the next step that should be undertaken is that of compiling lists of the more important persons in your area who are potential suspects. Make two lists, one of those likely to support the British, and another of those likely to support the Germans and Italians.[12]

Notably, the risk from those who might 'support the Germans and Italians' rarely featured in Mulvihill's reports, which were dominated by information on British or British-leaning residents. Detailed reports were sought from the intelligence officer network on each suspect and needed to include whether they were members of public bodies and whether they owned a telephone, a car or a boat or yacht. Most importantly, 'the whereabouts of all suspects' should be known 'at all times'. Mulvihill, in particular, set about 'compiling lists' and reports on those potential suspects, particularly those who were British or believed to be hostile to Irish interests.

A few examples of Mulvihill's reports to Florence O'Donoghue show the extent of hostility to British or Anglo-Irish residents in County Kerry, which endured from the War of Independence and earlier. Mulvihill monitored the movement of many with links to the British establishment. Among them was the McGillycuddy of the Reeks. A member of the Irish Senate and Kerry County Council and a supporter of Cumann na nGaedheal, he had been decorated for his service in the British Army in the First World War. In September 1940 Mulvihill told O'Donoghue: 'McGillycuddy of the Reeks has gone back to the British army.'[13] In a similar vein, a Captain Campbell Joseph O'Connor Kelly, a former British Army soldier, who was described as 'one of the most dangerous and efficient intelligence officers' operating in Kerry during the War of Independence, was closely observed by Mulvihill and his network of SIS men.[14] During the War of Independence, Mulvihill and the local IRA had spent a lot of time trying to target Kelly but each time they had an opportunity, 'he escaped'.[15] Kelly, later awarded the George Medal for his role in the British Army, was known to visit Lady Edith Gordon at Ard na Sídhe in Caragh Lake near Killorglin. In November 1940 Mulvihill reported: 'Captain Kelly, Caragh Lake: Is only in residence about one year, came there instead of a Major Matthews, is about six feet in height, fifteen stone weight, around sixty years of age, fresh, well liked locally, is said to be a native of Clare. Will supply more information re above on Friday next.'[16]

Closer to home for Mulvihill, the Godfrey family of Kilcolman Abbey, Milltown, was the subject of his attentions. The Godfreys had been landlords in the area for centuries and, even though they were a largely benign influence, politically, Mulvihill maintained a close eye on their movements:

> Mary Lady Godfrey, Kilcolman Abbey, Milltown: Sir John Godfrey is at present, I think, on Home Defence in England. He very seldom visited the place: two old maids in residence there at present. They have a very quiet life, and very few visitors ever call. Were never one of the actively hostile English group ... They never seemed to take any interest or part in politics and never went to the trouble of mixing up [*sic*] with the people. As far as I know they were never very hostile not even during 1920–21 period. D.M.[17]

A further communication from Mulvihill to O'Donoghue in November 1940 highlights not only the extent of the SIS intelligence network across the county but also how attuned Mulvihill was to the shifting political sands. Anyone considered pro-British or sympathetic to the Nazis was under suspicion but there was also a clear sectarian element to the work of the SIS, with those who were not Catholic or Irish being singled out for close scrutiny:

> Parson Thompson, The Rectory, Milltown: Protestant minister for Milltown-Castlemaine area. Bitterly anti-

Irish and anti-Catholic. Had to apologise for statements published in English paper some time in 1936 re the bad treatment of Southern Loyalists.

Lady Mary and Lady Eily Godfrey, Kilcolman, Milltown: Lady Mary, 70 years. Lady Eily, about 60 years ... they were never hostile but all connections are British. Giles, Denny Street, Tralee, one of the Orange Lodge, is agent for her.

Patrick O'Shea, Killorglin: About 65 years of age. Catholic, pro-British. Wool merchant, publican, has son officer in British army. Sons in L.D.F. Uncle to Dr Ryan's wife, was always bitterly hostile to Irish movement.

Huggards Hotel, Caragh Lake: Owned by Huggards of Waterville. Hotel very popular, public telephone, run by manageress Miss Bradshaw, a Catholic. No one staying there at present. Four men stayed there over the weekend, left today, Car No. ZA 3345 ... I understand the German Consul's family is at the 'Butler Arms' at Waterville presently.[18]

Gilbey, Tullig, Killorglin: About 34 years of age. Protestant, married? Got a motor car, a boat with outboard engine, seems to have spent good part of his time in U.S.A. Bought a farm of about 200 acres somewhere near Limerick City, about three weeks ago, has lot of it in

> grazing. He is Scotch and seems to have heaps of money. Seldom mixes with any young people.[19]

Despite the fears of invasion, and despite German plans for the occupation of Ireland under 'Operation Green', Ireland survived the Second World War without any coordinated incursion by a foreign power and with its military neutrality intact. The work of the SIS was at an end and Mulvihill's documented role in the organisation was locked away for decades in archives and not recognised until now. Though he and his former comrades were not forced to take up arms again during the Second World War, Mulvihill was as prepared as ever to fight for his country, particularly against the old enemy: 'If anyone thinks we would not have fought in 1940, they are making a hell of a mistake. They might have made a desert of the country, but we'd have made a desert of England also.'

+++

As the 1940s ended, Dan Mulvihill appeared, in his own words, for the 'first and last time' on an election platform. Many of Mulvihill's contemporaries had stepped into the political arena in the years after the Civil War, including IRA leaders like Tom McEllistrim, Fred Crowley, Thomas O'Donoghue and Paddy Cahill, with whom Mulvihill had been involved in ambushes at Glenbeigh, Lispole and elsewhere. One of those who embraced electoral politics and who Mulvihill knew better than most was Jack Flynn, his neighbour from Brackhill, with whom he had grown up and joined the fight for independence when they were teenagers. Flynn, as noted earlier, was elected to Kerry County Council in 1926 and joined Fianna Fáil. A charismatic and popular politician, he topped the poll in Kerry in the general election in 1932, in an election in which the party won five of the seven seats in the constituency. His performance showed how effective Fianna Fáil was at attracting former IRA commandants into the ranks and how they became the largest and strongest anti-Treaty party in the country.

Shortly before the 1943 general election, however, Flynn was mired in controversy when rumours circulated that he had fathered a child with a young woman outside of wedlock.[20] Flynn was expelled from Fianna Fáil as a result and did not contest the elections of 1943 and 1944. In a remarkable turnaround, however, and despite the controversy and the personal toll these events took on him, Flynn decided to stand in the 1948 general election as an independent candidate. Among those who supported his candidacy was Dan Mulvihill, who signed his nomination papers:

> Jack Flynn was expelled from Fianna Fáil party, a culmination of events over a few years. He did not go forward in the next election [1943 and 1944], and the war was over, I saw him slowly dying. The 1948 election came. I went to his house and forced him to go forward. He did not want to go. He was afraid of the people. At the first meeting I had to go up and introduce him. My first and last time on a platform. We had a fight on our hands, as

> most of his previous backers were part of the machine and worked for Fianna Fáil. I was not against F.F., I was backing a fellow who had been in the [flying] Column with me. I think I was always what they call a maverick.

The political gamble paid off and Flynn was elected as a non-party TD. He was later re-admitted to Fianna Fáil and remained a TD until 1957, when he was defeated in Kerry by his former IRA comrade John Joe Rice, who won a seat for Sinn Féin on an abstentionist platform. Dan Mulvihill supported and likely canvassed for votes for Flynn throughout his time in politics, as did Mulvihill's brother, Timothy (Todd), a chemist in Killorglin, and Thomas O'Connor of the Milltown IRA who later lived in Killorglin.[21] Dan Mulvihill would continue to be a much sought-after signatory for election nomination papers among Fianna Fáil politicians in Kerry, including his close friend Timothy 'Chub' O'Connor, a TD from 1961 to 1981 who was also a former IRA volunteer. While remaining outside of party politics, Mulvihill retained a political influence as a veteran of the fight for the Irish Republic. And though he never put his own name on a ballot paper and never wanted to become a politician, as his life progressed, he came into ever greater contact with politicians of all ranks and employed his effective political nous as he began to lobby and campaign for better rights and remuneration for the men and women who had fought for Irish freedom.

CHAPTER 12

'We are so fed up with charity'

DAN MULVIHILL'S POLITICAL SUPPORT for his friend and neighbour, Jack Flynn, opened a new phase of his life, one which would occupy a significant amount of his time in the decades which followed. Though he kept on farming the land at Brackhill and tried to embrace civilian life, the past continued to occupy much of his time. For many years, Mulvihill had been assisting his former comrades in their applications for pensions and allowances for their roles in events between 1916 and 1923. A range of payments for veterans of the Easter Rising and the War of Independence were provided for under a series of Pensions Acts, but it was only when Fianna Fáil came to power in the 1930s that members of the anti-Treaty IRA during the Civil War and members of Cumann na mBan became eligible for the payments. A number of Army Pensions Acts and Military Pensions Acts incorporated various amendments up until 1953. The application and verification process was often tedious, onerous and protracted, involving a lengthy application form, the provision of evidence and references to verify what was defined as 'active service', as well as interviews before an assessment board. The bar was set very high. For most of those who applied there was disappointment: of the 80,000 people who applied for pensions and allowances between 1924 and 1958, just over 18,000 were successful.[1] Mulvihill himself was awarded a military service pension for five years and ten months of active service on 15 February 1938, but most of his comrades – male and female – were not so fortunate.[2]

As a senior figure in the Kerry IRA for so long, Mulvihill was regularly approached by men and women in search of proof and references to confirm their involvement in the revolution. The application files of IRA and Cumann na mBan members, particularly those from within Mulvihill's brigade, are peppered with handwritten notes sent from Brackhill confirming that a particular combatant was involved, what their activities were and a comment on how critical they were to the fight against the Crown forces. One such case was Maria Shea from Mulvihill's neighbouring parish, about whom he testified:

> Mrs Maria McCarthy (*née* Shea) was a member of the Keel Cumann na mBan 1917 to 1924. She was one of the girls who provided for the Kerry No. 1 Brigade Col. from October 1920 to the Truce. They supplied them with food and cigarettes, carried their dispatches and did the washing for them, they could not have carried on without six or seven

> of those girls. They also in many cases removed arms and ammunition for members of [the] column. I know that Mrs McCarthy herself took arms and ammunition for me. Signed, Daniel Mulvihill, Batt. Adjt. 1921.[3]

In a similar vein, Mulvihill certified the active service of Mary 'May' O'Sullivan of Castledrum, who kept senior republicans like Pádraig Ó Siochfhradha (known by his pen-name 'An Seabhac' and later a senator and chairman of Kerry County Council) during the 'Tan time' when 'Kerry was in a blaze'.[4] O'Sullivan could, he wrote, 'be considered as one of the persons on whole time active services. This was due to the presence of Brigade Hut [the Hut] in Coy. Area ... I think that this lady is entitled to not alone full time service for that period but that she is also entitled to rank.' He provided similar testimonies in support of IRA men, as well as for countless relatives of those who died.

Mulvihill also made lists of those involved in combat in his area, something which proved crucial for the Department of Defence in verifying the bona fides of applicants. One of Mulvihill's comrades, Humphrey 'Free' Murphy, had previously proposed that local commanders should provide membership rolls and records of activities carried out by the brigades and their sub-units to assist the pension applications process. For example, Mulvihill provided a handwritten list of all of those involved in the Ballymacandy ambush of 1921, as well as a sketch of the site of the ambush and a full list of the Milltown Company of the IRA in July 1921, when the War of Independence ended.[5] He also contributed to the production of a detailed timeline of events in which the Kerry No. 2 Brigade was involved and against which pension assessors could verify the information provided by a particular applicant. The extent of this administrative work is clear from some of the documents in Mulvihill's private papers: in the 1930s, he compiled and maintained lists of applications and their status, cases which he usually discussed with other high-ranking former volunteers. One list from 1936 was titled: 'Files for discussion with Mr D. Cronin on 19/11/36 at 10.30am.' Denis Cronin from New Street, Killarney was a battalion lieutenant during the War of Independence.[6] The document points not only to Mulvihill's attention to detail and maintenance of copious records but also highlights, again, the extent of emigration among former IRA volunteers, many of whom were listed as residing abroad:

> 2875: Shanahan, Edm. Rchd. M.D. Farranfore, Co. Kerry. Statement promised not received. File brought forward.
>
> 4045: O'Sullivan, Florence, 164 Homestead Ave., Hartford, Conn., USA. Deferred case, again brought forward (3rd Battn, Kerry II).
>
> 6243: O'Dwyer, Daniel, Sunhill, Killorglin. In correspondence with Mr. Cronin re rank. Qualified.
>
> 6444: Moynihan, Michael, 685 East 140 St. New York. In correspondence with Mr. Cronin re list of keymen (E. Coy. 5th Bn. Kerry II).

> 16568: O'Brien, Bernard, 457 West 164 St. New York. Served with G. Coy, 3rd Bn. Kerry Il. Qualified. About £22.
>
> 22701: James O'Donoghue, Dromneavane, Kenmare. Statement promised by Mr. Cronin not received. File brought forward.

Throughout the 1930s and 1940s, Mulvihill continued to provide documentation to the Department of Defence and at an increasing rate as the eligibility for pensions and allowances was widened by successive governments. He had established himself not only as a go-to source of references, lists, maps and verifying documents but also as an authority on the military pensions legislation. This experience and expertise were about to be put to use on a much grander scale.

+++

Following his election as an Independent TD in 1948, Jack Flynn chose not to support his former party, Fianna Fáil – from which he had been expelled five years earlier – and instead voted to support the nomination of Fine Gael's John A. Costello as Taoiseach. In doing so, he helped Costello to form Ireland's first inter-party government consisting of Fine Gael, Labour, National Labour, Clann na Poblachta and Clann na Talmhan. Two years later, a prestigious position became available, and Flynn nominated his former IRA comrade for the post. Mulvihill was surprised but honoured when, in February 1950, he was appointed to the Advisory Committee within the Department of Defence which adjudicated upon the applications by former members of the IRA, Cumann na mBan, the National Army and other organisations for pensions, allowances and gratuities: 'Jack Flynn voted with the coalition [in 1948] and when the forming of [the] Pensions Board came up he nominated me, then told me. I could not see any crowd giving me a job.'

Mulvihill was appointed to the Advisory Committee on 6 February 1950:[7]

> There were a lot nominated and I got a bit of a shock when Sean Moran who was Assistant Secretary [Department of Defence] at the time called me and told me that I had got it.[8] They picked on Personal Records and in my case Army Verification. They asked M.J. Costello, and I got it on his recommendation.[9] It caused a lot of trouble in Kerry, as I was a well-known maverick. The work was very interesting as the files contained all the information of everything from 1916 to 1923.

Mulvihill also served as a member of the Board of Assessors – which was established under the Military Service Pensions Act, 1924 – at various times up to 1951. The function of the three-member board was to consider every application for a certificate of military service that was referred to them by the Minister for Defence, and to verify the military service of the applicant. The chairman of the board during much of Mulvihill's term was Art O'Connor, a former Sinn Féin TD and circuit court judge for

Cork city. Following his death in May 1950, the chair was taken by Eugene Sheehy, a senior counsel from Limerick and former judge advocate general of the Defence Forces. Mulvihill's fellow committee member was former National Army colonel Austin Brennan from County Clare.[10] That Mulvihill was just one of three members of such a notable committee was evidence of his reputation for diligent administrative work; his appointment was even more significant given the legislative requirement that at least one of the three members was to be a judge or a practising barrister of not less than ten years standing.

The board's work was tedious: applicants were required to appear before it in person and provide evidence under oath of their role in a particular organisation like Cumann na mBan, the National Army, the IRA or Fianna Éireann. The typed evidence would be placed on the applicant's file. The board then reported to the Minister for Defence on the extent, if any, of military service and the rank of the applicant and the appropriate number of years for pension purposes in accordance with the rates set out in the various Acts. The Military Service Pensions (Amendment) Act, 1949, enabled persons whose applications for service pensions under the Military Service Pensions Act of 1924 and 1934 had been rejected to send a petition in writing to the Board of Assessors or Referee through the Minister for Defence requesting the re-examination of their applications, which only added to the workload:

> We travelled to most of the counties and heard the cases there, and if possible visited the place where it (fight)

> took place. I still had my I.R.A. friends and two of them Kerry men were working in Dublin. Tom Mulvihill whose brother died Easter Week, and Sean Fuller [brother of Stephen], both related to me.[11] I used to stay a lot in the Castle Hotel [Dublin].[12] Donal O'Connor, the owner, had been interned with me in the Curragh. Paddy McLogan was Chief of Staff and when he stayed at the Castle, we would spend hours talking as we were old-time friends.[13]

Like so many aspects of the military pensions process over many decades, the system was intensely political, with Fianna Fáil TDs and ministers accused of showing preference to anti-Treaty applicants, and those in Fine Gael lobbied by and lobbying for those who had served in the National Army. On one occasion, Mulvihill was accused of political bias in his approach to a Kerry pension applicant. John Foley was a National Army private from Caragh Lake who was killed in Dublin during the Civil War in November 1922.[14] His parents received £100 compensation in 1923 and 'about £40' of a gratuity, which they considered 'a very small sum for a young man's life'.[15] When the late soldier's mother, Julia, became eligible for a dependant's pension payment in the 1950s, the claim was investigated by Mulvihill through his role with the Department of Defence. It was claimed that he didn't interview Mrs Foley about the veracity of her claim but 'went to local people who were cutting turf and made inquireys [*sic*] to know were they sure John Foley was in the National Army'. John Foley's brother, Patrick, was dubious of Mulvihill's investigation and motivations, telling Kerry Fine Gael TD Patrick Palmer that he was very 'suspicious that this was done for the purpose of creating a ring for getting Jack Flynn [Fianna Fáil TD for Kerry South] into it.' The allegation was that Mulvihill was attempting to secure credit (and votes) for his friend, Jack Flynn TD, if the application for a pension was successful. Regardless of the political charges, Mrs Foley was awarded an allowance in respect of her son's death in 1955.

Politics was often at play too when pensions boards and advisory committees were being formed: Mulvihill suspected that one Fine Gael minister was not keen on his membership of the Advisory Committee. Though it was a Fine Gael minister – Thomas F. O'Higgins – who had first appointed Mulvihill to that body with the support of Jack Flynn, Mulvihill was certain that another minister had him in his sights. Seán Mac Eoin, who had been chief of staff of the National Army and a member of the Blueshirts, was appointed Minister for Defence in the second inter-party government (1954–57) and Mulvihill was convinced that 'he wanted to get rid of me'. 'Sean Mac Eoin was Minister [for Defence][16] – he wanted to get rid of me. Tadhg Forbes, our Referee, died suddenly, and he [Mac Eoin] got his chance.'

Tadhg Mac Firbhisigh (Forbes), a former member of Fianna Éireann and the Gaelic League, was a district court judge who had been a member of the Advisory Committee with the Pensions Board since 1944.[17] When he died suddenly in 1954, Mac Eoin 'got his chance' to appoint a new committee. Yet

Mulvihill remained a member of the Advisory Committee until the end of 1955, having served for almost five years.

+++

If his work on military pension applications in the 1950s taught Mulvihill anything, it was that the vast majority of those who applied were denied any money. With less than a quarter of applicants securing payments in the period between 1924 and 1958, the high rate of refusal created what Diarmaid Ferriter described as a 'chronicle of great disappointment' and an indictment of what many perceived as 'cold, harsh bureaucracy'.[18] That bureaucracy infuriated Mulvihill, particularly in his older years, as he pursued successive governments in an effort to get them to respect and acknowledge the Old IRA and the members of Cumann na mBan for their service in the fight for Irish independence. During the late 1960s and the early 1970s, the Old IRA in the 1st Southern Division lobbied successive governments for an increase in their pensions. As a former adjutant with the division, Mulvihill became one of the key protagonists in that campaign. He exploited his IRA contacts across the country and advocated for improved payments and recognition for the 'veterans of '21'. He began to write extensive correspondence to the Department of Defence, as well as to Kerry Fianna Fáil TDs Timothy 'Chub' O'Connor and John O'Leary.[19] The correspondence from Mulvihill emphasises not only a sense of disillusionment with Fianna Fáil and the political parties generally but also a sense of anger and betrayal about the way that former IRA veterans felt they were being treated. In a stinging indictment of Fianna Fáil, written to O'Connor in 1971, Mulvihill excoriated the government of which 'Chub' was a backbencher:

> All F.F. [Fianna Fáil] ever gave the I.R.A. was the usual charity they were allowed to give, free travel, free E.S.B., free television, all for the over 70s and all with a string. They gave widows' pensions to the widows of [the] Civil Service pensioners last year, and as there was a lot of money saved in I.R.A. pensions, they decided they'd extend it and make them happy. It will be extended next year to all Local Government employees.
>
> Our crowd are nearly finished. They will be down to around the thousand next year as I suppose they are hardly worth considering.
>
> We will be having another meeting [of the Old IRA] shortly, a big one. I enjoy listening to some of the boys ... Slán agus beannacht. D. Mulvihill.[20]

Successive ministers in successive governments were also on the receiving end of invective and criticism from Mulvihill. Jerry Cronin from Fermoy became Minister for Defence in 1970 following the Cabinet reshuffle, which was prompted by the Arms Crisis and which involved the sacking of his predecessor, Neil Blaney. Cronin was in the defence ministry for three years and was no stranger to the role of men and women during the War of Independence and the Civil War. His father, Seán, had served in the IRA alongside Liam Lynch, and his uncle, Arthur

Mulcahy, was shot dead during an engagement with Crown forces in 1921. During his term as minister, Cronin was more preoccupied with the threat of the IRA of the early 1970s – as the situation deteriorated in Northern Ireland – than he was with the IRA of the 1920s. He showed no inclination to indulge the demands of Mulvihill and his peers, as a letter to Kerry TD John O'Leary in 1971 betrays:

> With further reference to your representations at the instance of Mr. Daniel Mulvihill ... that the pensions of all grades of the Old I.R.A. should be increased, you will appreciate that military service pensions have been increased on nine occasions in the last ten years ... Any further increase in military service pensions could be considered only in the context of Budget increases in pensions generally ...[21]

Mulvihill was typically unimpressed and infuriated:

> The pensions granted in 1934 have gone up 3½ times. The cost of living 10 times. We didn't ask to have them raised to [the] cost of living. What we asked them to do would balance out financially at the end of the year as there will be another thousand dead and the really big pensioners would get no increase.

Mulvihill also suggested that ministers were under the thumb of their civil service masters:

> I was the only one of the lot [Old IRA] with experience of [the] Civil Service. I told them the ministers would consult the Civil Service. I don't think there's a minister making a decision on his own ... The Civil Service love giving out charity, anything with a string and a means test and we are so fed up with charity ... I won't say any more. Give the Minister this to read and see what his reactions are. You know they'll [the Old IRA] go out to F.G. and Labour if there's an election. D.M.[22]

Timothy 'Chub' O'Connor also came in for plenty of criticism from Mulvihill. Although Mulvihill signed his nomination papers at almost every general election that 'Chub' contested, and though the pair remained good friends, the Fianna Fáil TD was often reminded that the party wouldn't have become the success it was without the Old IRA:

> I was looking at the Paper today and I saw about the Ministerial [pay] rises. I got a Dead Fit of laughing. Out of a thousand, they took three hundred and fifty off me. I want you to do the following for me. Go to Bobby Molloy [Minister for Defence] and say to him is it a fact that you are taxing what's left of the old I.R.A. They are all over eighty ... They are the fellows that put us here [Fianna Fáil in government]. I think the people of the country will be interested to hear about it.[23]

The responses to this and similar letters do not survive.

+++

The limited correspondence with other Old IRA leaders across the country that remains in the Mulvihill papers highlights how the surviving combatants of the War of Independence were deeply moved by events in Northern Ireland in the late 1960s and early 1970s. It is clear that many like Mulvihill saw a need for the veterans of the 1920s to comment publicly as a collective body on what was becoming 'The Troubles' in the Six Counties. Mulvihill contacted others in neighbouring divisions and drafted a statement as a commentary and set of demands from the veterans of the War of Independence about the developing situation. Though the draft statement does not survive, some of the feedback from his comrades does and proves that Mulvihill, like so many others, was deeply perturbed by the plight of nationalists and Catholics north of the border in the late 1960s and early 1970s. A reply to Mulvihill in 1971 by Paddy O'Brien of Mallow, a former head of the Cork No. 4 Brigade of the IRA, highlights not only a collective disgust about the fact that Ireland remained partitioned but also a realism that the Old IRA held a decreasing influence in the Ireland of the 1970s. O'Brien told Mulvihill:

> I feel it would not be wise to commit ourselves [to a public statement] ... representing the 1st Sth. Div. Old IRA ... so far we have never had a fully represented meeting from the 10 Brigades in the 1st Sth. Div. 1) What could we do, if we are told as most likely we would be, that we only

> represent something that have [*sic*] been dying a slow death for the past 50 years. 2) We never accepted partition as a solution ... The Treaty was forced on us by the threat of immediate and terrible war ... Now that a section of the people, who have suffered for 50 years as a result of what was forced on them by the threat of violence, have been forced to use violence to get their position before the eyes of the world, [they] are being condemned by Church and State. We might find something to say in support of those who were compelled to resort to violence.[24]

Throughout the 1970s, Mulvihill continued to make efforts or organise the Old IRA as an advocate group and have them contribute to political discourse. Among his correspondents was Tom Barry, one of Ireland's most high-profile republican leaders, whom he had once dismissed in correspondence as 'a crank'. Best known for leading the Kilmichael ambush in County Cork in 1920, Barry was born in Killorglin in 1897, the son of an RIC officer who was based in the town. Though never directly involved in the war in Kerry, Barry remained a heroic figure for many republicans in Kerry and beyond. As chief of staff of the IRA in 1937, he spearheaded plans for an incursion into Northern Ireland, though it never materialised. Mulvihill remained in contact with Barry in later years and he leaned on him for support for attempts to reorganise the Old IRA and campaign for better pension payments and entitlements. Both Mulvihill and Barry were born in 1897 and were entering their eighties as they continued to lobby on behalf of their comrades. His advancing years notwithstanding, Barry pledged his support to Mulvihill's efforts in 1976 even if he was not very optimistic about success:

> I would of course be prepared to help in any way the Volunteers who are now old and some indeed very much in need. But I am not very hopeful that anything can be done with the present set up in Govt [Fine Gael–Labour coalition] where a half a dozen top bureaucrats are running the country. If you send me a short note stating all the subjects to be discussed [at a meeting] and the names of those to be invited, I will write you by return. I am due to unveil memorials in Cavan on the 30th inst., in Co. Mayo on the following Sunday, June 6th and to deliver the oration on the 50th anniversary of Crossbarry on the 13th or 20th June. Le meas mór, Tom Barry.[25]

Mulvihill also lobbied Moss Twomey, who had been IRA chief of staff until 1936 and served time in jail in the 1930s. Like Barry, Twomey believed that the passage of time would restrict efforts to mobilise the Old IRA around a campaign for improved rights and supports:

> Some weeks ago, I was interested in the same idea, but when I found some of those whom I consulted not willing to endorse the full campaign, I dropped it. I doubt if the influence of 'has-beens' is very much now. When I had

> in mind a statement, I specifically wished to call to Vets [veterans] to take the initiative for having funds raised in their districts [for Northern Ireland], if that was not being done already ... I do feel that any support, even moral support, will be welcomed.[26]

Mulvihill remained deeply upset and frustrated that it was only 'moral support' that many of his former comrades and fellow citizens could provide to those who were suffering the terror of Ireland's newest 'Troubles'. Save for a few social gatherings of veterans, the men and women of the War of Independence never mobilised or mobilised others in any meaningful way, despite the best efforts of one of its most effective and dynamic leaders. With a melancholy tone, Mulvihill noted in his memoir: 'the years were drifting by and all the old fellows were going one by one'.

CONCLUSION

'I am still unchanged'

THE CLOSING PASSAGES OF Dan Mulvihill's memoir are a series of short and pithy – and at times cantankerous – reflections on the world around him as he entered his ninth decade. The commentary on the issues of the day is intensely political – and party political, at that – and demonstrates not only a disillusionment with and sense of betrayal by the political system but also a sense of disappointment and regret about what he and his brothers and sisters in arms had failed to achieve. He was none too impressed with the 'vindictive' coalitions of Fine Gael and Labour in the 1970s and early 1980s, and suggested that the Fine Gael leader and Taoiseach Liam Cosgrave, son of W.T., was a chip off the old block:

> A Coalition Government [is] coming.[1] We knew that there were plenty brains there and plenty patriotism in Opposition. They were paper tigers, small brains and no patriotism. Everything bad the Fianna Fail party had been

> doing, they set out to out-do it and in every case did so. F.F. had been bad but never vindictive as the new set-up was. They have crawled to the British and asked – following in his father's footsteps and like his father he has not much control over his Ministers. The unfortunate thing is the present set have got a bee in their bonnet. They have gone completely vindictive over the Provos [Provisional IRA] ...[2]

The context for Mulvihill's completion of his manuscript in the early 1980s, as well as the voluminous correspondence he generated at this time – be it letters to Old IRA comrades, local TDs or government ministers – was the rapidly deteriorating situation in Northern Ireland. The cycle of brutal sectarian violence deeply moved and perturbed many like Mulvihill, who felt both angered and powerless about the plight of the nationalist and Catholic communities. He was particularly disturbed when Taoiseach Jack Lynch dismissed two of his ministers over an alleged plot to import arms to be used to defend those communities: Mulvihill believed that Lynch 'panicked and we had the sacking of the Ministers and the Arms Trial'.[3] The reaction of Fianna Fáil leaders and successive Irish governments to the plight of the nationalist people in Northern Ireland saddened and infuriated Mulvihill in equal measure. He was exasperated by the decision of Fianna Fáil, in particular, to 'draw back' from meaningful intervention:

> The North came out and we left them down. We stood idly by. The first time in all our history that we pulled

> back. They asked for arms to defend themselves and we could not give them. They might shoot some of the English who were coming to beat them up. Why did we draw back for the first time in our history? When this history will come to be written, what will from 1969 to Exodus be like? How will the leaders be judged?

Mulvihill was dismayed by most of the political leaders of the 1970s and 1980s but he reserved praise for two Irish leaders whom he considered heroes. Patrick Pearse, signatory of the Proclamation of the Irish Republic and probably the best-known of the leaders of the Easter Rising, was a hero but so too was the man Mulvihill smuggled out of Dublin at the beginning of the Civil War:

> Pádraig Pearse saw a nation dying and tried to start a fire. He knew he was going to die and as time was running out on Good Friday [1916], he paid tribute to the men who had fought for the four previous days and asked those who came after them to remember them. They did for a few short years. One saving feature, there was one man who through thick and thin remained Irish, and was and is, though he is dead hated for it. Don't anyone ever think that there were any Superman [*sic*] in the 1916 to 1921 period. There was none. The nearest we ever got was Éamon De Valera and do you think, for a second, he is not hated by a lot of people still?

It is perhaps no accident that Mulvihill concluded one of the very final versions of his memoir with an extract from one of Pearse's poems, a composition which remains synonymous with the development of the Irish nation. 'Mise Éire' (I am Ireland) was Pearse's 1912 lament in which an old woman celebrates Ireland's glorious ancient past but bemoans the new political establishment and expresses her shame at their failure to completely free Ireland from the shackles of British subjugation. Two of the poem's lines were chosen as Mulvihill's final words:

Mór mo náir:
Mo chlann féin a dhíol a máthair

(Great is my shame:
My own children who sold their mother)

Many of Pearse's generation, in Mulvihill's mind, had 'sold their mother' and betrayed and abandoned the Irish republic. Mulvihill felt the same about the political establishment of his later years. As a younger man, he had been confident that a united Ireland could be achieved. 'I know that the British are going to go. That's certain,' he wrote. But he became more pessimistic as the years progressed. In a letter to a friend written on 9 January 1984, exactly a year to the day before he died – the last of the surviving correspondence in his personal archives – Mulvihill was crestfallen but immovable in his principles:

> I am still unchanged, but as far as my dream of living to see a united Ireland is concerned [it] is like the glory of Greece ... gone with the wind ... I'm eighty-seven, pair of bad legs to make up for the good ones I once had. Seán McEntee died last evening, 95[4] ... I wrote a lot of stuff, burned it all. A X [ex] priest has just gone off with one I wrote. One Man's Ireland. Covering from 1915 to 1977. Just my story ... I think I'll stop. Time is running out ... Hand shaking, reason for machine [typewriter] and mistakes. D.M.[5]

Into old age, Mulvihill remained convinced that there was a need to maintain an organisation to step up when a united Ireland was in sight and to step in when the nationalists of Northern Ireland faced oppression and hardship: 'I still wanted to see a nucleus that could be fallen back on if the time arrived.' This ambition was never fully realised by Mulvihill or the veterans of the War of Independence, men and women who, like Dan and Katie Mulvihill, always deeply regretted the partition of the country and the enduring presence of British troops on Irish soil. So perhaps, in his eighties and in deteriorating health, and having failed to mobilise or organise his old comrades to a common purpose, Mulvihill believed there was one final way to make a stand, to set out what he believed, to document the sacrifices the men and women of his generation had made for Ireland. He would commit his story – warts and all – to paper and, through it, inspire a new generation of those who believe in the Irish Republic, a republic he devoted his life to and which he fought for with pen as well as sword.

ENDNOTES

INTRODUCTION

1 The author is grateful to Stephen Rae for sharing these recordings, which are now retained in the Local History and Archives Unit of the Kerry County Library in Tralee.
2 Interview with Dan Mulvihill by David and Stephen Rae (1984), courtesy of Stephen Rae.
3 See 'Con Casey' in Uinseann Mac Eoin, *Survivors* (Argenta Publications, 1980), pp. 370–8.
4 Ibid., p. 377.
5 Cooney was IRA chief of staff in 1925–26 and not in the 1930s, as stated by Mulvihill.
6 See Owen O'Shea, *Ballymacandy: The Story of a Kerry Ambush* (Merrion Press, 2021).
7 Billy Mullins, *Memoirs of Billy Mullins: Veteran of the War of Independence* (Kenno, 1983).
8 Jeremiah Murphy, *When Youth Was Mine* (Mentor Books, 1998).
9 Seamus O'Connor, *Tomorrow Was Another Day: The Irreverent, Humorous Earthy Memories of an Irish Rebel Schoolmaster* (Anvil Books, 1970).

1: 'GREAT FIGHTERS AND MEN OF SPLENDID PHYSIQUE'

1 Seán Moraghan, *Days of the Blackthorn: Faction Fighters of Kerry* (Mercier Press, 2020), p. 60.
2 Moraghan, *Days of the Blackthorn* gives a full account of faction fighting in Kerry in the nineteenth century.
3 Ibid., p. 46.
4 Ibid., p. 61.
5 Ibid., p. 64.

6 *Kerry Evening Post*, 7 July 1834.
7 Bureau of Military History, Witness Statement (hereafter BMH WS) 938, Dan Mulvihill, p. 1.
8 Central Statistics Office, Census of 1901, www.cso.ie.
9 Ibid.
10 BMH WS 938, Dan Mulvihill, p. 1.
11 Ibid.
12 'Jeremiah O'Donovan Rossa – the Fenian leader's connections with Milltown',: https://owenoshea.ie/jeremiah-odonovan-rossa-the-fenian-leaders-connections-with-milltown/.
13 Horatio Herbert Kitchener, 1st Earl Kitchener (who was born in Ballylongford, County Kerry in 1850) was British Secretary of State for War and was killed on 5 June 1916 when the ship HMS *Hampshire*, which was travelling to Russia, struck a German mine off the Scottish coast, killing 737 passengers.
14 The Serpentine is a large lake in Hyde Park in London which is used for recreation.
15 Bridget McAuliffe, Mary McAuliffe and Owen O'Shea (eds), *Kerry 1916: Histories and Legacies of the Easter Rising – A Centenary Record* (Irish Historical Publications, 2016), p. 233.
16 Ibid., p. 240.
17 Gordon Revington, 'Kerry's Patriot Dead: Mulvihill, Shortis, O'Connor and The O'Rahilly' in ibid., pp. 141–50.
18 Comment from an earlier draft of Mulvihill's memoir, kindly provided by Stephen Rae.
19 *The Keystone Cops* was a slapstick comedy series produced as silent films between 1912 and 1917. *The Exploits of Elaine* was a film serial first released in 1914.
20 From an undated note: Mulvihill Papers, P64, University College Dublin Archives (hereafter UCDA).
21 *Kerry Weekly Reporter*, 18 April 1914.
22 *The Cork Examiner*, 17 October 1914.
23 *Kerry Weekly Reporter*, 22 November 1913.
24 *Kerry Evening Star*, 24 November 1913.
25 McAuliffe et al., *Kerry 1916*, p. 247.
26 *The Kerry Evening Post*, 16 May 1916.
27 Mary McAuliffe, 'Kerry and the Irish Volunteers, 1913–1917' in McAuliffe et al., *Kerry 1916*, p. 65.
28 BMH WS 938, Dan Mulvihill, p. 2.
29 Mary McAuliffe, '"Loyalty and courage": Kerry women and Cumann na mBan, 1914–1917' in McAuliffe et al., *Kerry 1916*, p. 79.

30 Milltown District Council, 6th Battalion, Kerry II Brigade: CMB/121, Cumann na mBan Nominal Rolls, Military Service Pension Collection (hereafter MSPC), held at the Military Archives (hereafter, MA).
31 Pension application of Katie Mulvihill, MSP34REF59896, MSPC.
32 BMH WS 938, Dan Mulvihill, p. 2.
33 Tom O'Connor in Cormac K.H. O'Malley and Tim Horgan (eds), *The Men Will Talk to Me: Kerry Interviews by Ernie O'Malley* (Mercier Press, 2012), p. 146.
34 A native of Quin, County Clare, John Joseph Hassett played inter-county hurling for Cork between 1916 and 1921.
35 John Borgonovo, 'Cork', in John Crowley, Donal Ó Drisceoil, Mike Murphy and John Borgonovo (eds), *Atlas of the Irish Revolution* (Cork University Press, 2017), p. 558.
36 Stephen O'Neill (1895–1966) was vice O/C with the Cork No. 3 Brigade and was jailed during the Civil War. He was second in command at the Kilmichael ambush in November 1920.
37 Jim 'Spud' Murphy (1900–76) from Clonakilty took part in ambushes at Kilmichael and Crossbarry.
38 John 'Flyer' Nyhan (1892–1934) from Clonakilty was captain of the Cork No. 1 Brigade. During the Civil War he was shot six times but survived.
39 A reference to outbreaks of fighting during the War of Independence.
40 This is taken to mean that students at the college were suspended or expelled.

2: 'CALM BEFORE THE STORM'

1 Map of Kerry IRA brigades and companies, in John Crowley, Donal Ó Drisceoil, Mike Murphy and John Borgonovo (eds), *Atlas of the Irish Revolution* (Cork University Press, 2017), p. 545. The 6th Battalion was part of the Kerry No. 1 Brigade until the spring of 1921 when it transferred to Kerry No. 2.
2 BMH WS 1,000, James Cronin, p. 2.
3 BMH WS 938, Dan Mulvihill, p. 5.
4 D.M. Leeson, *The Black and Tans: British Police and Auxiliaries in the Irish War of Independence* (Oxford University Press, 2011), p. 4.
5 Charlie and Tom Daly (or Dálaigh) from Knockaneacoolteen, Firies were members of a prominent republican family in Kerry. Charlie Daly (1896–1923) fought with the 2nd Northern Division during the War of Independence. He was captured by National Army forces and executed at Drumboe in County Donegal on 14 March 1923 along with Seán

Larkin, Dan Enright and Timothy O'Sullivan. Tom Daly (1898–1939) was active during the War of Independence and went on hunger strike while in jail during the Civil War. In November 1924 he stood as the Sinn Féin candidate in a by-election in Donegal, winning 42 per cent of the vote.

6 This incident occurred at Pallis, Beaufort on a steep road overlooking the main road between Killarney and Killorglin and adjacent to Beaufort Bridge on the River Launce.

7 Negley Farson, *The Way of a Transgressor* (Edward Gaskell Publishers, 2001), p. 263.

8 James Scott Negley Farson (1890–1960) was an American adventurer and author. He published *The Way of a Transgressor* in 1936.

9 T. Ryle Dwyer, *Tans, Terror and Troubles: Kerry's Real Fighting Story 1913–1923* (Mercier Press, 2001), p. 17.

10 William Sheehan, 'The British Army in Ireland', in Crowley et al., *Atlas of the Irish Revolution*, p. 368.

11 David M. Leeson, 'The Royal Irish Constabulary, Black and Tans and Auxiliaries', in ibid., p. 381.

12 The RIC barracks in Milltown was located at the corner of Main Street and Castlemaine Road. Following a number of incidents the barracks moved briefly to another property on Main Street before the RIC were relocated to nearby Killorglin. The sergeant in charge was James Collery, who was killed at the Ballymacandy ambush on 1 June 1921: see Owen O'Shea, *Ballymacandy: The Story of a Kerry Ambush* (Merrion Press, 2021), passim.

13 BMH WS 938, Dan Mulvihill, p. 3.

14 Patrick (Paddy) Cahill (1884–1946) from Tralee was O/C of the Kerry No. 1 Brigade during the War of Independence. He was a Sinn Féin TD for Kerry from 1921 to 1927.

15 BMH WS 1067, Daniel Healy, p. 4.

16 Major Leeson-Marshall to his daughter, May, 3 November 1920: Diary of Major Markham Richard Leeson-Marshall, Muckross House Research Library, Killarney.

17 Kilderry is a townland to the south of Milltown. The ambush was launched from Kilderry Wood.

18 Crossley Tender trucks were a common mode of transport for the Crown forces.

19 BMH WS 938, Dan Mulvihill, p. 4.

20 This area spans from Inch in west Kerry through Milltown and Castlemaine in mid-Kerry as well as parts of the Iveragh Peninsula and the parishes of Glencar and Beaufort near the MacGillycuddy's Reeks.

21 BMH WS 1,011, Patrick Garvey, pp. 27–8.

3: 'THE GOOD HOUSES'

1 Marnie Hay, 'Na Fianna Éireann,' in John Crowley, Donal Ó Drisceoil, Mike Murphy and John Borgonovo (eds), *Atlas of the Irish Revolution* (Cork University Press, 2017), p. 173.
2 Mulvihill to Pensions Board, 11 November 1940: Pension application of Joan O'Sullivan, MSP34REF31796, MSPC.
3 Pension application of Joan O'Sullivan, MSP34REF31796, MSPC.
4 'Sworn evidence of Mrs Joan O'Sullivan (*née* O'Brien) given before Verifying Officers on 22.1.1941', MSP34REF31796, MSPC.
5 Collins Papers, IE-MA-CP-04-40, MA. Constable Patrick Bergin was a native of County Carlow. An ex-soldier, he joined the RIC in April 1920 as a recruit to the Black and Tans. He was known to be sympathetic to the IRA and often provided them with information: Owen O'Shea, *Ballymacandy: The Story of a Kerry Ambush* (Merrion Press, 2021), pp. 152–3.
6 Collins Papers, IE-MA-CP-04-40, MA.
7 Ibid.
8 Owen O'Shea, *No Middle Path: The Civil War in Kerry* (Merrion Press, 2022), pp. 125–7.
9 Following the killing of an IRA member, Joe Taylor, in Glencar in February 1921, and a number of attacks on the barracks in Glencar, it was abandoned by the RIC, with members being redeployed to barracks at Milltown and Killorglin: O'Shea, *Ballymacandy*, pp. 67–8.
10 Caherconree (Cathair con Raoi) is a mountain peak in the Sliabh Mish Mountains on the Dingle Peninsula where a promontory fort is located. Cú Roí Mac Dáire was the King of Munster in Irish mythology.
11 Cú Chulainn, a warrior hero in Irish mythology.
12 The Bealach Béama and Bealach Óisín are two mountain passes located within the MacGillycuddy's Reeks.
13 John Richard (Jack) Shanahan (1900–71) a member of the IRA from Castleisland was shot during a police raid on the Daly home on 9 May 1921: see MA, MSP34REF2874.
14 George Gilmore (1898–1985) from Dublin was a leading figure in the IRA and a member of the communist-leaning Republican Congress in the 1930s. It is likely that he knew Tom Dálaigh, who was a member of the IRA Army Council in the 1930s.
15 Seán MacBride (1904–88) was a prominent political figure in twentieth-century Ireland. He opposed the Treaty and was jailed during the Civil War. He was a founder member of the left-wing republican group

Saor Éire in 1931 and was briefly IRA chief of staff in 1936 before being called to the Bar in 1937. In 1946 he founded a new republican party, Clann na Poblachta, and was Minister for External Affairs from 1948 to 1951.

16 Pension application of Katie Mulvihill, MSP34REF59896, MSPC.

17 O'Shea, *No Middle Path*, pp. 146–7.

18 Joe Taylor of Lyranes, Glencar was O/C of the 6th Battalion and died on 27 February 1921 after being beaten and shot by the RIC at his home.

19 Jim (Séamus) Taylor (1897–1923) of Lyranes, Glencar was killed by Free State forces during the Civil War in March 1923.

20 Frank Grady (1895–1923) from Glenbeigh was shot dead by Free State army captain Michael 'Tiny' Lyons on 11 March 1923: O'Shea, *No Middle Path*, p. 79.

21 There is no record of a Michael Dwyer being killed during the Civil War so this may be a reference to Michael Ahern who was killed by Free State forces in October 1922.

22 Tom O'Connor was seriously wounded during fighting in County Limerick in July 1922.

23 Seán Bartholomew 'Bertie' Scully (1897–1961) from Shanacashel, Glencar was a member of the 6th Battalion of the IRA and was wounded in County Limerick during the Civil War. His brother, Liam Scully (1892–1920), was killed during an IRA assault on Kilmallock RIC Barracks in May 1920.

24 The Wade brothers were members of a republican family from Killorglin. Their sisters, Chrissie and Amelia, were members of Cumann na mBan. Amelia was married to Alexander 'Sonny' Mason, O/C of the Kiltallagh Company of the IRA.

25 Maureen (Máirín) O'Shea (b. 1896) was a member of Killorglin Cumann na mBan and was also active in London and Liverpool during the War of Independence: MSP34REF64001, MSPC.

26 Chrissie and Amelia Wade, see note 24.

27 O'Shea, *Ballymacandy*, pp. 59–60.

28 Pension application of Katie Mulvihill, MSP34REF59896, MSPC.

4: 'UNTIL HE BLED TO DEATH'

1 BMH WS 379, Jeremiah Mee, p. 10.

2 Owen O'Shea, *Ballymacandy: The Story of a Kerry Ambush* (Merrion Press, 2021), pp. 47–8.

3 BMH WS 882, Thomas McEllistrim, p. 24.

4 The cottages referred to are on the current Laune View estate overlooking the main bridge in Killorglin.
5 Callinafercy is a townland between Milltown and Killorglin which had a boundary with Castlemaine Harbour. It was used as a crossing point for volunteers from the Hut and from west Kerry, which enabled them to avoid the roads and the likelihood of detection by Crown forces.
6 O'Shea, *Ballymacandy*, p. 68.
7 Ibid.
8 BMH WS 1,000, James Cronin, pp. 4–5.
9 *Kerry People*, 19 March 1921.
10 Tom O'Connor in Cormac K.H. O'Malley and Tim Horgan (eds), *The Men Will Talk to Me: Kerry Interviews by Ernie O'Malley* (Mercier Press, 2012), p. 132.
11 *Kerry People*, 19 March 1921.
12 For an account of the Lispole ambush, see Noel Ó Murchú, *War in the West, 1918–1923: The Struggle for Irish Independence on the Dingle Peninsula Based on the Testimonies of Those Who Fought the Campaign* (Mountain Range Press, 2020), pp. 182–207 and a locally published account by Mícheál Ó Móráin, *Luíochán Lios Póil: The Lispole Ambush* (2021).
13 BMH WS 1,000, James Cronin, p. 7.
14 The Ashe family of Kinard including Thomas Ashe, who had died while being force-fed at Mountjoy Prison.
15 Tommy Hawley (1897–1921) from Tralee was a member of the A Company of the 1st Battalion of the Kerry No. 1 Brigade.
16 Thomas M. Ashe (1897–1921), a first cousin of the Thomas Ashe who died in Mountjoy in 1917, was a native of Kinard and a lieutenant in the Lispole Company.
17 Jim Daly from Castlegregory was injured at Lispole but survived. He was a brother-in-law of Tadhg Brosnan (1891–1971), a senior figure in the IRA in west Kerry throughout this period.
18 The Maum is a mountain pass between Camp and Inch/Castlemaine.
19 A stony outcrop near Caherconree named after the Irish mythological character.
20 BMH WS 938, Dan Mulvihill, pp. 9–10.
21 *The Kerryman*, 1 May 1971.
22 For more on Lynch, see Gerard Shannon, *Liam Lynch: To Declare a Republic* (Merrion Press, 2023).
23 Ibid., p. 111.
24 Michael Hopkinson, *The Irish War of Independence* (Gill & Macmillan, 2014), p. 128.

25 Bridget McAuliffe, Mary McAuliffe, and Owen O'Shea (eds), *Kerry 1916: Histories and Legacies of the Easter Rising – A Centenary Record* (Irish Historical Publications, 2016), pp. 228–9 and passim.
26 O'Shea, *Ballymacandy*, pp. 78–80.
27 Bertie Scully in O'Malley and Horgan (eds), *The Men Will Talk to Me*, p. 164.
28 Ibid., p. 153.
29 Hopkinson, *The Irish War of Independence*, p. 128.
30 Pension application of Katie Mulvihill, MSP34REF59896, MSPC.

5: 'MAD TO GET THE CHANCE'

1 'Unlikely ambush position was deliberately chosen near Castlemaine' by Edward Gallagher in *With the IRA in the Fight for Freedom: 1919 to the Truce* (Mercier Press, 2010), p. 414.
2 Interview with Ned Horan by David and Stephen Rae (1984), reproduced with the kind permission of Stephen Rae. Horan was later a senator representing Clann na Talmhan.
3 The Mulvihill, Cronin and Flynn homesteads were a short distance from each other in the townland of Brackhill.
4 Timothy Brick, Edward Barrett and Denis Quirke were all members of the Milltown Company of the IRA.
5 The road which runs west from Castlemaine on the Dingle Peninsula through the parish of Keel.
6 Diary of Major Leeson-Marshall, 27 February, 27 April 1921, Muckross House Research Library.
7 D.M. Leeson, *The Black and Tans: British Police and Auxiliaries in the Irish War of Independence* (Oxford University Press, 2011), p. 28.
8 Owen O'Shea, *Ballymacandy: The Story of a Kerry Ambush* (Merrion Press, 2021), p. 86.
9 Gregory Ashe in Cormac K.H. O'Malley and Tim Horgan (eds), *The Men Will Talk to Me: Kerry Interviews by Ernie O'Malley* (Mercier Press, 2012), p. 121.
10 For more on the Ballymacandy ambush, see O'Shea, *Ballymacandy*.
11 The Kiltallagh Company included IRA members from Castlemaine and Kiltallagh. Alexander 'Sonny' Mason was Company Captain. His wife, Amelia (*née* Wade), a native of Killorglin, was a member of Cumann na mBan. Mason's neighbour and cousin, William (Bill) Burke of Ballygamboon Lower, was 1st lieutenant.
12 Gallagher in *With the IRA in the Fight for Freedom*, p. 418.

13 Kilderry (on the Killorglin side of Milltown) was the location of an ambush of Black and Tans by the IRA on 1 November 1920.
14 Jerry Myles from Moyderwell, Tralee. His brother, Billy, was killed during the Civil War. Myles was later secretary of Kerry GAA and died in 1950.
15 Dr Daniel Sheehan (1882–1971) of Glen Ellen, Milltown was medical officer for the local IRA. His father, Jeremiah Sheehan, had been MP for East Kerry from 1885 to 1895.
16 Bryan (Bryannie) O'Brien from Ardcanaught, Castlemaine was O/C of the Keel IRA, members of which participated in the Ballymacandy ambush. O'Brien's brother, Michael, was Bishop of Kerry from 1927 to 1952.
17 BMH WS 788, Sean 'Bertie' Scully, p. 26.
18 Gregory Ashe in *The Men Will Talk to Me*, p. 121.
19 Leeson, *Black and Tans*, pp. 139–40.
20 BMH WS 788, Sean 'Bertie' Scully, p. 26.
21 A crossing point on the River Laune near Killorglin.

6: 'THE TRUCE WAS ON, AND WE COULD NOT BELIEVE IT'

1 Eunan O'Halpin, 'Counting Terror: Bloody Sunday and "The Dead of the Irish Revolution"' in David Fitzpatrick (ed.), *Terror in Ireland: 1916–1923* (Lilliput, 2012), p. 152.
2 Owen O'Shea, *Ballymacandy: The Story of a Kerry Ambush* (Merrion Press, 2021), pp. 50–1.
3 *Kerry People*, 16 July 1921; *Irish Independent*, 10 July 2021; *The Irish Times*, 10 July 2021.
4 Mulvihill is incorrect: there were three casualties. Richard (Dick) Shanahan and Jack Prendiville from Castleisland and Jack Flynn from Gortatlea were killed by the Crown forces in Castleisland on 10 July 1921.
5 Jeremiah Murphy, *When Youth Was Mine* (Mentor Books, 1998), p. 171.
6 Sinéad Joy, *The IRA in Kerry, 1916–1921* (Collins Press, 2005), p. 108.
7 Cited in Martin Moore, *The Call to Arms: Tom McEllistrim and the Fight for Freedom in Kerry* (An Gabha Beag, 2016), p. 82.
8 *Kerry People*, 23 July 1921.
9 Diary of Major Leeson-Marshall, 18 July 1921, Muckross House Research Library.
10 Ibid., 31 August 1921.
11 Lady Edith Gordon, *The Winds of Time* (J. Murray, 1934), p. 189.
12 Ibid., pp. 189–91.

13 Tom Doyle, *The Civil War in Kerry* (Mercier Press, 2008), p. 46.
14 Joy, *The IRA in Kerry*, pp. 109–10.
15 Pension application of John P. Heffernan, MSP34REF10816, MSPC.
16 Bertie Scully in Cormac K.H. O'Malley and Tim Horgan (eds), *The Men Will Talk to Me: Kerry Interviews by Ernie O'Malley* (Mercier Press, 2012), p. 154.
17 *The Cork Examiner*, 29 November 1921.
18 *Irish Independent*, 9 August 1921.
19 Owen O'Shea, *No Middle Path: The Civil War in Kerry* (Merrion Press, 2022), pp. 8–10.
20 *An t-Óglach*, 16 July 1921.
21 Ibid., 14 October 1921.
22 Pension application of Annie Mary O'Connor, MSP34REF6000, MSPC.
23 Pension application of Thomas Corcoran, MSP34REF31668, MSPC.
24 Note from Seán Brosnan, F Company, 4th Battalion, IRA, undated; pension application of Thomas Rohan, MSP34REF13932, MSPC.
25 Moore, *The Call to Arms*, p. 83; Statement of James Coffey, Battalion Training Officer, Kerry No. 2 Brigade; Application of James Coffey, MSP34REF4356, MSPC.
26 Information from Dr John Knightly.
27 Pension application of Katie Mulvihill, MSP34REF59896, MSPC.
28 Letter from Dan Mulvihill in the pension file of Michael Casey, MSP34REF56399, MSPC.
29 Pension application of Mary Riordan (*née* Casey), MSP34REF62133, MSPC.
30 Tim Horgan, *Dying for the Cause: Kerry's Republican Dead* (Mercier Press, 2015), p. 249.
31 Pension application of Maurice Casey (Snr), 1D158, MSPC.
32 Ibid.
33 Ibid.

7: 'THINGS ARE GETTING WORSE EVERY DAY'

1 Draft truce terms dated 9 July 1921: National Archive of Ireland via Digital Repository of Ireland.
2 Ibid.
3 Mark Duncan, 'Endgame 1921: Towards Truce and Treaty in Ireland': www.rte.ie/centuryireland/articles/endgame-1921-towards-truce-and-treaty-in-ireland.
4 Statement of costs, 25 November 1921: Mulvihill Papers, P64/9(2), UCDA.

5 Chief Liaison Officer to Mulvihill, 31 October 1921: Mulvihill Papers, P64/7(1), UCDA.

6 *The Cork Examiner*, 26 October 1921. Lancaster was later a commissioner of the police in The Bahamas where he died in 1965: theauxiliaries.com.

7 Emmet Dalton (1898–1978) was born in the United States. He joined the British Army in 1915 and fought on the Western Front including at the Battle of Ginchy in 1916 and later in Palestine. On returning to Dublin, he joined the IRA with his brother, Charlie, in 1919 and took part in the War of Independence. He became a major general in the new National Army in 1922, leading the assault on the Four Courts which began the Civil War.

8 While senior IRA commander Seán Mac Eoin was in jail in Mountjoy, Michael Collins made several attempts to rescue him. On this occasion, 14 May 1921, Dalton, wearing a British Army uniform, tried but failed to rescue Mac Eoin after driving into Mountjoy in a commandeered armoured car.

9 Papers of Captain Daniel Mulvihill, P64, UCDA. The papers were deposited by Shane Mulvihill in 1983.

10 This is a reference to the burning of the coastguard station at Ballydavid. The building had been set alight by the IRA and damage was also caused to adjacent houses and other buildings: Noel Ó Murchú, *War in the West, 1918–1923: The Struggle for Irish Independence on the Dingle Peninsula Based on the Testimonies of Those Who Fought the Campaign* (Mountain Range Press, 2020), p. 250.

11 Mulvihill to O/C Kerry No. 2, 10 November 1921, Mulvihill Papers, P64/1(1), UCDA.

12 For more on the big houses of Kerry in this period, see John Knightly, 'The Destruction of the Big House in Kerry, 1920–1923' in Jane O'Hea O'Keeffe (ed.), *The Big House in Kerry: A Social History* (Irish Life and Lore, 2022), pp. 1–22.

13 Kerry No. 2 Brigade to Liaison Offices, Buttevant, Cork: Mulvihill Papers, P64/1(4), UCDA.

14 Knightly, 'The Destruction of the Big House', p. 17.

15 Chief Liaison Officer to Mulvihill, 11 November 1921: Mulvihill Papers, P64/1(6), UCDA.

16 Adjutant, Kerry No. 2 Brigade to Mulvihill, 18 November 1921: Mulvihill Papers, P64/1(10), UCDA.

17 J.E. Dalton to Mulvihill, 18 January 1922: Mulvihill Papers, P64/6(10), UCDA. There was no recorded outcome of the case.

18 Kerry No. 2 Brigade to Mulvihill, 28 November 1921: Mulvihill Papers, P64/5(13), UCDA.

19 District Inspector, Listowel to Mulvihill, 23 November 1921: Mulvihill Papers, P64/1(18), UCDA.
20 Capt. Lancaster to Mulvihill, 20 December 1921; Capt. Lancaster to Mulvihill, 23 December 1921: Mulvihill Papers, P64/1(27) and (30), UCDA.
21 Capt. Lancaster to Mulvihill, 26 December 1921: Mulvihill Papers, P64/1(41), UCDA.
22 Mulvihill note, 21 December 1921: Mulvihill Papers, P64/1(28), UCDA.
23 Mulvihill to Kerry No. 3 Brigade, 12 January 1922: Mulvihill Papers, P64/2(11), UCDA.
24 Liaison Officer to Mulvihill, 26 December 1921: Mulvihill Papers, P64/1(25), UCDA.
25 John Murray to Mulvihill, 7 November 1921: Mulvihill Papers, P64/5(1), UCDA.
26 Ibid.
27 Emmet Dalton, Liaison Officer to Mulvihill, 13 January 1922: Mulvihill Papers, P64/2(13), UCDA.
28 Statement of Constable 'S.A.S.B., Castleisland', 14 November 1921: Mulvihill Papers, P64/3(15), UCDA.
29 Report to Mulvihill, 1 December 1921: Mulvihill Papers, P64/7(26), UCDA.
30 W. Doolin, Chief Secretary's Office to Chief Liaison Officer, 26 January 1922: Mulvihill Papers, P64/8(16), UCDA.
31 Copy of report received from Kenmare, 18 November 1921: Mulvihill Papers, P64/3(19), UCDA.
32 Kerry No. 3 Brigade to Mulvihill, 15 December 1921: Mulvihill Papers, P64/3(74), UCDA.
33 Emmet Dalton, Liaison Officer to Mulvihill, 25 January 1922: Mulvihill Papers, P64/2(24), UCDA.
34 Mulvihill to Chief Liaison Officer, 21 January 1922: Mulvihill Papers, P64/2(25), UCDA.
35 The jail is a reference to Ballymullen Barracks, which was the British Army headquarters in Tralee.
36 John Joe Sheehy (1897–1980) from Tralee was an active republican from a young age as a member of Fianna Éireann and the IRA. He took the anti-Treaty side during the Civil War and served time in jail in the 1940s. Sheehy played inter-county football for Kerry, winning four All-Ireland senior titles, captaining Kerry in 1926 and 1930.
37 Mulvihill report, 21 January 1922: Mulvihill Papers, P64/2(38), UCDA.
38 Mulvihill to Chief Liaison Officer, 21 January 1922: Mulvihill Papers, P64/2(39), UCDA.

39 Unsigned note to Mulvihill, 7 November 1921: Mulvihill Papers, P64/3(4), UCDA.
40 T. O'Hanrahan, D.I. to Mulvihill, 9 November 1921: Mulvihill Papers, P64/3(10), UCDA.
41 Henn Street is now Plunkett Street.
42 Constable Charles F. Ednie (25), a native of Edinburgh died in this incident, which records date to 2 February 1922.
43 *Irish Independent*, 3 February 1922.
44 Mulvihill to Chief Liaison Office, 7 March 1922: Mulvihill Papers, P64/8(42), UCDA.
45 Mulvihill to Chief Liaison Office, 7 March 1922: Mulvihill Papers, P64/8(46), UCDA.
46 Note of Dan Mulvihill, 16 December 1921: Mulvihill Papers, P64/3(66), UCDA.

8: 'THE DAY THE SPLIT STARTED'

1 Gerard Shannon, *Liam Lynch: To Declare a Republic* (Merrion Press, 2023), pp. 150–1.
2 Caitríona Crowe (ed.), *Guide to the Military Service (1916–1923) Pensions Collection* (Óglaigh na hÉireann, 2012), p. 95.
3 Tom O'Connor in Cormac K.H. O'Malley and Tim Horgan (eds), *The Men Will Talk to Me: Kerry Interviews by Ernie O'Malley* (Mercier Press, 2012), p. 138.
4 Owen O'Shea, *No Middle Path: The Civil War in Kerry* (Merrion Press, 2022), p. 19.
5 Shannon, *Liam Lynch*, pp. 161–2.
6 John Borgonovo, 'IRA Conventions', in John Crowley, Donal Ó Drisceoil, Mike Murphy and John Borgonovo (eds), *Atlas of the Irish Revolution* (Cork University Press, 2017), p. 671.
7 For Liam Lynch, see Shannon, *Liam Lynch*, op cit. For Florence O'Donoghue, see John Borgonovo (ed.), *Florence and Josephine O'Donoghue's War of Independence: A Destiny That Shapes Our Ends* (Irish Academic Press, 2006), p. 196.
8 Seán Moylan (1889–1957), a native of Kilmallock, Co. Limerick, was a senior figure in the IRA throughout this period. He was a TD for a number of Cork constituencies between 1932 and 1957, serving as a minister in several Fianna Fáil governments. Ernie O'Malley (1897–1957) from Castlebar, Co. Mayo was active in the Volunteers and the IRA in Dublin and was assistant chief of staff of the anti-Treaty IRA during

the Civil War. He published several well-known books, including *On Another Man's Wound* and *The Singing Flame*, and interviewed many of the combatants from the Irish revolutionary period.

9 Joe Griffin (1900–67) from Tralee was a member of the A Company of the IRA in the town and he took part in the burning of the Custom House in Dublin in May 1921. He was with Harry Boland when he was mortally wounded during the Civil War. Later a civil servant, he was controller of prices during the Second World War and was a director of *The Irish Press*.

10 Borgonovo (ed.), *Florence and Josephine O'Donoghue's War of Independence*, p. 196. Roderick (Rory) O'Connor (1883–1922) from Dublin was among 200 anti-Treaty IRA members who occupied the Four Courts in Dublin on 14 April 1922. Liam Mellows (1892–1922) was a leading figure in the anti-Treaty IRA.

11 J.J. 'Ginger' O'Connell (1887–1944) was deputy chief of staff of the National Army. On 26 June 1922, he was kidnapped by anti-Treaty forces in reprisal for the arrest of anti-Treaty IRA officer Leo Henderson. The kidnapping precipitated the shelling of the Four Courts two days later.

12 O'Shea, *No Middle Path*, p. 28. Full details of the casualties that occurred in Kerry are provided in Hélène O'Keeffe, John Crowley, Dónal Ó Drisceoil, John Borgonovo and Mike Murphy (eds), *Atlas of the Irish Civil War: New Perspectives* (Cork University Press, 2024).

13 T. Ryle Dwyer, *Tans, Terror and Troubles: Kerry's Real Fighting Story 1913–1923* (Mercier Press, 2001), p. 353.

14 O'Shea, *No Middle Path*, pp. 29–30.

15 Donal O'Callaghan (1891–1962) was lord mayor of Cork from 1920 to 1924, succeeding Terence MacSwiney who died on hunger strike in October 1920. He was elected in 1920 and voted against the Anglo-Irish Treaty. In June 1923 he was sent to the US by Éamon de Valera to replace Laurence Ginnell as a republican envoy.

16 BMH WS 938, Dan Mulvihill, p. 15.

17 David McCullagh, *De Valera: Volume I: Rise (1882–1932)* (Gill Books, 2017), p. 290.

18 Ibid.

19 Harry Boland (1887–1922) was a close friend and ally of Michael Collins. A former president of the IRB he opposed the Treaty as a TD for Mayo South–Roscommon South. He was shot by National Army soldiers on 31 July 1922, as they were attempting to arrest him, and died in hospital the following day.

20 The barracks at Beggars Bush was a British Army base that was taken over by the IRA in January 1922.

21 Eoin O'Duffy (1890–1944) was a general in the National Army and later the commissioner of the Civic Guard (later An Garda Síochána). He was the leader of the Blueshirt movement in the 1930s and was the first leader of the Fine Gael party.

22 Presumably Tom O'Connor of Milltown, who was injured during fighting in Kilmallock in County Limerick in July 1922.

23 Shannon, *Liam Lynch*, p. 195.

24 Sean Boyne, *Emmet Dalton: Somme Soldier, Irish General, Film Pioneer* (Irish Academic Press, 2014), p. 201.

25 McCullagh, *De Valera: Rise*, p. 294.

26 Crowe, *Guide to the Military Service*, p. 95.

27 Michael Hopkinson, *Green Against Green: The Irish Civil War* (Gill & Macmillan, 2004), pp. 164–5.

28 Eight hundred National Army soldiers under Emmet Dalton arrived by sea at Cork between 8 and 10 August 1922.

29 The railway bridge in Mallow was blown up by anti-Treaty forces on 9 August 1922.

30 A sounder was used to communicate telegraphic messages.

31 Robert Erskine Childers (1870–1922) was a London-born author who fought in the Boer War before joining republican organisations in Ireland. He was a TD for Kildare–Wicklow (1921–22) and though a signatory of the Treaty, he became one of its most vocal critics. He was tried for possession of a pistol and executed in November 1922.

32 Deasy published an account of his life in the IRA in 1973 entitled *Towards Ireland Free: The West Cork Brigade in the War of the Independence, 1917–1921* (Mercier Press, 1992) as well as an account of the Civil War, *Brother Against Brother* (Mercier Press, 1982).

33 Florence O'Donoghue was a historian and published several books including *No Other Law: The Story of Liam Lynch and the Irish Republican Army, 1916–1923* (Irish Press Ltd, 1954).

34 Joseph O'Connor (1880–1959) was a member of 'The Squad' under Michael Collins during the War of Independence and was later a Cumann na nGaedheal senator.

35 John Francis (Seán) Hyde (1897–1977) from Ballinhassig played inter-county hurling for and did intelligence work for Michael Collins during the War of Independence.

36 Dr Con Lucey (1899–1929) was an IRA Director of Medicine and was an aide to Liam Lynch during the Civil War. He played inter-county hurling and football for Cork.

37 Lieutenant Colonel Gerald Bryce Ferguson Smyth was the RIC Divisional Commissioner for Munster. He was shot dead by the IRA at the Cork & County Club on 17 July 1920.

38 RIC District Inspector Oswald Swanzy was killed by members of the Cork No. 1 Brigade on 22 August 1920 in Lisburn, County Antrim. His killing was a reprisal for the killing of Tomás MacCurtain, Lord Mayor of Cork, on 20 March 1920.

39 Jackie Bolster and Dick Willis were members of the Mallow Battalion of the IRA who instigated a high-profile raid on Mallow RIC Barracks on 28 September 1920.

40 For the shooting of Henry Wilson, see Ronan McGreevy, *Great Hatred: The Assassination of Field Marshal Sir Henry Wilson MP* (Faber & Faber, 2022).

9: 'LAMB TO THE SLAUGHTER'

1 Gavin Foster, 'The Civil War in Kerry in history and memory' in Maurice J. Bric (ed.), *Kerry: History and Society.* Interdisciplinary Essays on the History of an Irish County (Geography Publications, 2020), p. 475.

2 Pension application of Katie Mulvihill, MSP34REF59896, MSPC.

3 Ibid.

4 For an account of the role played by Marguerite Fleming in this period, see Tim Horgan, *Fighting for the Cause: Kerry's Republican Fighters* (Mercier Press, 2018), pp. 43–57.

5 Johnny 'Machine Gun' Connor (1899–1955) from Farmers' Bridge was a prominent figure in the Kerry No. 1 Brigade during the War of Independence and he was jailed during the Civil War. He was elected a Clann na Poblachta TD for Kerry North in 1954 and was killed in a car accident in December 1955: see Owen O'Shea and Gordon Revington, *A Century of Politics in the Kingdom: A County Kerry Compendium* (Merrion Press, 2018), pp. 95–106.

6 See Horgan, *Fighting for the Cause*, pp. 185–98.

7 BMH WS 938, Dan Mulvihill, p. 14.

8 Major General Paddy O'Daly (1888–1957) was a senior figure in the Dublin Guard of the National Army and assumed control of the Command on 1 January 1923. He arrived in Kerry on 2 August 1922 with 450 troops on board the *Lady Wicklow* at Fenit. He oversaw some of the worst violence and killings of the Civil War in Kerry.

9 Dorothy Macardle, *Tragedies of Kerry* (Emton Press, 1924), p. 29.

10 Jeremiah Murphy, *When Youth Was Mine* (Mentor Books, 1998), p. 248.

11 It is not clear if this is a reference to Florence O'Donoghue of Rathmore who had left the IRA at the beginning of the Civil War. It may refer to an earlier incident or to another IRA member.

12 It is not clear whether Mulvihill was referring to Hannon or Martin here.

13 Murphy was executed by Colonel David Neligan on the steps of the Great Southern Hotel on 27 September 1922, ostensibly in reprisal for the deaths of the two soldiers at Brennan's Glen.

14 Tim Horgan, *Dying for the Cause: Kerry's Republican Dead* (Mercier Press, 2015), p. 208.

15 May Daly in Cormac K.H. O'Malley and Tim Horgan (eds), *The Men Will Talk to Me: Kerry Interviews by Ernie O'Malley* (Mercier Press, 2012), p. 96.

16 Owen O'Shea, *No Middle Path: The Civil War in Kerry* (Merrion Press, 2022), pp. 77–8.

17 For more on this incident, see 'Looting, kidnap, murder and mayhem: A dramatic and tragic four days in one Kerry village during Ireland's Civil War': https://owenoshea.ie/looting-kidnap-murder-and-mayhem/.

18 For a full list of all civilian casualties in Kerry, see Hélène O'Keeffe, John Crowley, Donal Ó Drisceoil, John Borgonovo and Mike Murphy (eds), *Atlas of the Irish Civil War: New Perspectives* (Cork University Press, 2024), pp. 442–80.

19 For more on the executions, see Arthur Mathews, *Walled in by Hate: Kevin O'Higgins, His Friend and Enemies* (Merrion Press, 2024), pp. 119–22.

20 O'Shea, *No Middle Path*, p. 76.

21 Dan Browne from Meelin, Co. Cork was a member of the Cork No. 2 Brigade.

22 Patrick Long, 'Patrick O'Keeffe', *Dictionary of Irish Biography*: www.dib.ie/biography/okeeffe-patrick-paudeen-o-caoimh-paraig-a6827.

23 The Dublin home of President Cosgrave was the subject of an arson attack on 13 January 1923; the seven-year-old son of Seán McGarry, a pro-Treaty TD, died following an arson attack on the family home on 10 December 1922.

24 Oriel House was the headquarters of the counter-insurgency police, the Criminal Investigations Department (CID) during the Civil War.

25 A Papal Count, George Plunkett (1851–1948) was Minister for Foreign Affairs, 1919–21 and father of Joseph Plunkett, one of the leaders of the Easter Rising.

26 Dr James Ryan (1892–1970) was a TD for Wexford from 1918 to 1922 and 1923 to 1965, and was a minister in all Fianna Fáil governments from 1932 to 1965.

27 P.J. Ruttledge (1892–1952) was a TD for Mayo from 1921 to 1952 and was a minister in several portfolios in the Fianna Fáil governments from 1932.

28 Eamon Donnelly (1877–1944) from Armagh was elected an abstentionist member of the Northern Ireland Parliament in 1925 and was later a Fianna Fáil TD for Laois–Offaly.

29 Seán Russell (1893–1940) from Dublin held senior positions in the IRA during the War of Independence and the Civil War. He was chief of staff of the IRA in 1938–39 and collaborated with Nazi Germany.

30 Brian O'Higgins (1882–1963) was a poet and writer and was a TD for Clare from 1918 to 1927.

31 Peadar O'Donnell (1893–1986) from Donegal was a socialist and writer who was elected a TD in 1923. He was later a founder member of Saor Éire and joined the republican militia during the Spanish Civil War.

32 Bernard (Ben) Brady (1903–49) was a Donegal IRA leader who was a TD from 1932 to 1949.

33 Peadar Duignan (1898–1955) was a TD for Galway West from 1951 to 1954.

34 Tipperary native Andy Cooney (1897–1968) was appointed O/C of the Kerry No. 1 Brigade in 1921 and was later chief of staff of the IRA (1925–26).

35 Cited in Horgan, *Fighting for the Cause*, pp. 273–4.

36 O'Shea, *No Middle Path*, pp. 82–106.

37 *The Irish Press*, 5 January 1938.

38 O'Shea, *No Middle Path*, pp. 109–11.

39 Owen O'Shea, 'The most violent county: Civil War deaths in Kerry': www.rte.ie/history/civil-war-fatalities/2024/0304/1435938-the-most-violent-county-civil-war-deaths-in-kerry/.

40 Joseph Stynes (1903–91) played inter-county football for Dublin in 1922 and 1923 while he was on the run as an IRA volunteer. He had been a steward at Croke Park on Bloody Sunday in 1920. He played on the New York team which defeated Kerry in New York in 1927 and was active in the Irish Northern Aid Committee (NORAID), which campaigned for an Irish Republic in the United States.

41 *Éire*, 10 November 1923.

42 Billy Mullins, *Memoirs of Billy Mullins: Veteran of the War of Independence* (Kenno, 1983), p. 163.

43 Austin Stack to Winifred Gordon, 24 October 1923, Papers of Austin Stack, MS 22,398/14, National Library of Ireland (hereafter NLI).

44 O'Shea, *No Middle Path*, passim.

10: 'WE RAIDED ONCE A MONTH'

1 For more on the 1923 election in Kerry, see Owen O'Shea, '"The only hope was to work the Treaty": Local newspaper coverage of the 1923 general election in County Kerry', in Elaine Callinan, Mel Farrell and Thomas Tormey (eds), *Vying for Victory: The 1923 General Election in the Irish Free State* (UCD Press, 2023), pp. 63–76.
2 BMH WS 938, Dan Mulvihill, p. 1.
3 Ibid.
4 Owen O'Shea, *No Middle Path: The Civil War in Kerry* (Merrion Press, 2022), passim.
5 'Report from Captain Tomás Ó Dálaigh, Kerry Command to IRA headquarters, January 1925', Papers of Moss Twomey, P69/99/12-13, UCDA.
6 Passport of Daniel Mulvihill: Mulvihill Papers, Miscellaneous items, P64, UCDA.
7 This is probably a reference to the Forest Preserves of Cook County in Chicago, a national state park.
8 Brian Hanley, *The IRA, 1926–1936* (Four Courts Press, 2002), p. 12.
9 Eunan O'Halpin, *Defending Ireland: The Irish State and Its Enemies Since 1922* (Oxford University Press, 1999), p. 78.
10 Extract from Police Report on Sinn Féin Ard Fheis, 1931 (6 October 1931), Department of Justice Files, JUS/2007/56/119, NLI.
11 Constitution and Rules of The Irish Workers' and Farmers' Republican Party, Department of Justice Files, JUS/2007/56/119, NLI.
12 Bishop O'Brien to the Clergy of the Diocese, 1931: Bishop O'Brien Papers, Statutes, Kerry Diocesan Archives.
13 Hanley, *The IRA*, pp. 124–5.
14 See Owen O'Shea, '"We are almost on the lip of the volcano": The Blueshirts in County Kerry, 1933–35', *Journal of the Kerry Archaeological and Historical Society*, series 2, vol. 22 (2022), pp. 53–78.
15 Ibid., pp. 64–5.
16 Hanley, *The IRA*, p. 16.
17 *The Kerryman*, 18 January 1985.
18 *The Times* (London), 12 July 1938.
19 *The Kerryman*, 18 January 1985.

11: 'BITTERLY ANTI-IRISH AND ANTI-CATHOLIC'

1 Eunan O'Halpin, *Defending Ireland: The Irish State and Its Enemies Since 1922* (Oxford University Press, 1999), p. 162.

2 Ibid., p. 153.
3 Ibid., p. 164.
4 It is understood that this is Peter Browne of the Currow Company of the Kerry No. 2 Brigade.
5 John Borgonovo (ed.), *Florence and Josephine O'Donoghue's War of Independence: A Destiny That Shapes Our Ends* (Irish Academic Press, 2006), passim.
6 Ibid., pp. 205–6.
7 O'Halpin, *Defending Ireland*, p. 166.
8 Borgonovo, *Florence and Josephine O'Donoghue's War of Independence*, p. 206.
9 Ballingarraun is located near Cloghane on the northern side of the Dingle Peninsula.
10 G2 Staff, Southern Command, Cork, 5 November 1940: Mulvihill Papers, P64, UCDA.
11 Ibid.
12 Handwritten instructions from Mulvihill to Intelligence Officers, 9 September 1943: Mulvihill Papers, P64, UCDA.
13 Mulvihill to Florence O'Donoghue, 6 September 1940, Florence O'Donoghue Papers, MS 31,345/2/28, NLI.
14 BMH WS 1,413, Tadhg Kennedy, p. 33.
15 Typed note in Mulvihill's papers, undated: Mulvihill Papers, P64, UCDA.
16 Mulvihill to Florence O'Donoghue, 5 November 1940, Florence O'Donoghue Papers, MS 31,345/2/34, NLI.
17 Mulvihill to Florence O'Donoghue, 2 November 1940, Florence O'Donoghue Papers, MS 31,345/2/33, NLI.
18 Eduard Hempel was German Minister (or Consul) to Ireland between 1937 and 1945. It was Hempel who formally, and controversially, received the condolence of Taoiseach Éamon de Valera following Hitler's death in May 1945. In an interview in 2011, Hempel's daughter, Liv, referred to childhood holidays in Waterville and other parts of Ireland: *The Irish Times*, 14 May 2011.
19 Mulvihill to Florence O'Donoghue, 25 November 1940, Florence O'Donoghue Papers, MS 31,345/2/47, NLI.
20 John O'Leary, *On the Doorsteps: Memoirs of a Long-Serving TD* (Irish Political Memoirs, 2015), p. 44; Owen O'Shea and Gordon Revington, *A Century of Politics in the Kingdom: A County Kerry Compendium* (Merrion Press, 2018), pp. 51–61.
21 O'Shea and Revington, *A Century of Politics in the Kingdom*, p. 59.

12: 'WE ARE SO FED UP WITH CHARITY'

1 Marie Coleman, 'The Military Service Pensions Collection', in John Crowley, Donal Ó Drisceoil, Mike Murphy and John Borgonovo (eds), *Atlas of the Irish Revolution* (Cork University Press, 2017), p. 885.

2 Pension application of Dan Mulvihill, MS34REF4800, MSPC.

3 Note from Dan Mulvihill, 17 February 1941: pension application of Maria McCarthy, MSP34REF7824, MSPC.

4 Note from Mulvihill, 22 November 1941: pension application of Mary (May) O'Sullivan, MSP34REF8597, MSPC.

5 List of members of the Milltown Company, 6th Battalion, Kerry No. 2 Brigade: RO109, MSPC.

6 Pension application of Denis Cronin, MSP34REF23014, MSPC.

7 Caitríona Crowe (ed.), *Guide to the Military Service (1916–1923) Pensions Collection* (Óglaigh na hÉireann, 2012), p. 95.

8 John James (Seán) Moran was a life-long civil servant who became assistant secretary in the Department of Defence in 1942.

9 Michael Joseph Costello from County Tipperary was an intelligence officer with the IRA in his locality and later became director of intelligence and a major general in the National Army.

10 Crowe, *Guide to the Military Service*, p. 85.

11 Tom Mulvihill was a brother of Michael Mulvihill from Ardoughter, Ballyduff in north Kerry, who was killed during the Easter Rising in Dublin. Seán Fuller, a brother of Stephen Fuller, remained active in the IRA after the Civil War and was involved in the IRA bombing campaign in England at the beginning of the Second World War (information courtesy of Dr Richard McElligott).

12 The Castle Hotel on Gardiner Row in Dublin was bought by Donal O'Connor in 1956.

13 Paddy McLogan (1899–1964) from County Armagh was president of Sinn Féin from 1950 to 1952 and from 1954 to 1962. He had been on hunger strike with Thomas Ashe in Mountjoy in 1917 and was an abstentionist MP for South Armagh.

14 Pension application of William Foley: 2D57, MSPC.

15 Patrick Foley to P.W. Palmer TD, 5 July 1954: 2D57, MSPC.

16 Seán Mac Eoin (1893–1973) was a member of Fine Gael and Minister for Justice (1948–51) and Minister for Defence (1951 and 1954–57) and a TD for Longford from 1921 to 1965. Known as the 'Blacksmith of Ballinalee', he was a senior IRA leader in his native county during the War of Independence and supported the Treaty in the vote in the Dáil in 1922.

17 Crowe, *Guide to the Military Service*, p. 91.
18 Diarmaid Ferriter, *A Nation and not a Rabble: The Irish Revolution, 1913–1923* (Profile Books, 2015), pp. 22, 333.
19 Timothy 'Chub' O'Connor was a Fianna Fáil TD for Kerry South from 1961 to 1981; John O'Leary was a Fianna Fáil TD for Kerry South from 1966 to 1997.
20 Mulvihill to Timothy O'Connor TD, 26 July 1971: MSPC, W34C336 Dan Mulvihill.
21 Minister for Defence to John O'Leary TD, 1 September 1971: MSPC, W34C336 Dan Mulvihill.
22 Mulvihill to John O'Leary TD, 2 July 1971: MSPC, W34C336 Dan Mulvihill.
23 Mulvihill to Timothy 'Chub' O'Connor TD, 5 December 1979: MSP34REF4800, MSPC.
24 P. O'Brien, Liscarroll, Mallow to Mulvihill, 23 September 1971: Mulvihill Papers, P64, UCDA.
25 Tom Barry to Mulvihill, 13 May 1976: Mulvihill Papers, P64, UCDA.
26 Moss Twomey to Mulvihill, 23 September 1971: Mulvihill Papers, P64, UCDA.

CONCLUSION

1 A coalition government involving Fine Gael and Labour, under Taoiseach Liam Cosgrave, was in office between 1973 and 1977.
2 The Provisional IRA (nicknamed the Provos) emerged from a split in the IRA in December 1969.
3 In 1970 ministers Charles Haughey and Neil Blaney were sacked following allegations that they had conspired to import arms for the IRA in Northern Ireland.
4 Belfast native and long-serving TD Seán MacEntee (1889–1984) was an IRA leader and served in several Fianna Fáil governments, including as Tánaiste under Taoiseach Seán Lemass (1959–66). He was, in fact, ninety-four years old at the time of his death.
5 Letter to Mike (name and details not specified) from Mulvihill, 9 January 1984: Mulvihill Papers, P64, UCDA.

INDEX